Daily WRITING & EDITING Practice

Fabrice Wilmann

First published in 2020, reprinted in 2022 (twice)

Insight Publications Pty Ltd
3/350 Charman Road
Cheltenham Victoria 3192
Australia

Tel: +61 3 8571 4950
Fax: +61 3 8571 0257
Email: books@insightpublications.com.au

www.insightpublications.com.au

Daily Writing and Editing Practice Book 1 / Fabrice Wilmann

ISBNs:
9781922378088 (print)
9781922378255 (digital)

Cover design, internal design & layout by Gisela Beer
Additional contributions by Robert Beardwood, Nick Heynsbergh, Melanie Napthine & Mariano Trevino
Educational consulting by Kim Hislop & Caitlin Penrose
Editing by Janice Bird
Proofreading by Julia Carlomagno

Printed by Markono Print Media Pte Ltd

Introduction

Daily Writing and Editing Practice Book 1 provides forty weeks of ten-minute daily activities that target the key English skills of writing and editing.

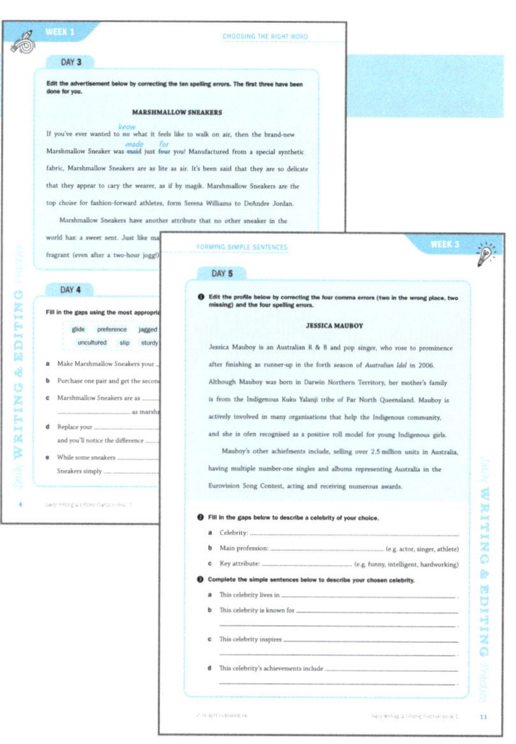
WEEK 1 CHOOSING THE RIGHT WORD

DAY 3

Edit the advertisement below by correcting the ten spelling errors. The first three have been done for you.

MARSHMALLOW SNEAKERS

If you've ever wanted to no what it feels like to walk on air, then the brand-new Marshmallow Sneaker was maid just four you! Manufactured from a special synthetic fabric, Marshmallow Sneakers are as lite as air. It's been said that they are so delicate that they appear to cary the wearer, as if by magik. Marshmallow Sneakers are the top choise for fashion-forward athletes, form Serena Williams to DeAndre Jordan.

Marshmallow Sneakers have another attribute that no other sneaker in the world has: a sweet sent. Just like ma… fragrant (even after a two-hour jogg!)

DAY 4

Fill in the gaps using the most appropri…

glide preference jagged uncultured slip sturdy

a Make Marshmallow Sneakers your …
b Purchase one pair and get the secon…
c Marshmallow Sneakers are as … as marsh…
d Replace your … and you'll notice the difference …
e While some sneakers … Sneakers simply …

FORMING SIMPLE SENTENCES WEEK 3

DAY 5

1 **Edit the profile below by correcting the four comma errors (two in the wrong place, two missing) and the four spelling errors.**

JESSICA MAUBOY

Jessica Mauboy is an Australian R & B and pop singer, who rose to prominence after finishing as runner-up in the forth season of *Australian Idol* in 2006. Although Mauboy was born in Darwin Northern Territory, her mother's family is from the Indigenous Kuku Yalanji tribe of Far North Queensland. Mauboy is actively involved in many organisations that help the Indigenous community, and she is ofen recognised as a positive roll model for young Indigenous girls.

Mauboy's other achiefments include, selling over 2.5 million units in Australia, having multiple number-one singles and albums representing Australia in the Eurovision Song Contest, acting and receiving numerous awards.

2 **Fill in the gaps below to describe a celebrity of your choice.**
a Celebrity: ……
b Main profession: …… (e.g. actor, singer, athlete)
c Key attribute: …… (e.g. funny, intelligent, hardworking)

3 **Complete the simple sentences below to describe your chosen celebrity.**
a This celebrity lives in ……
b This celebrity is known for ……
c This celebrity inspires ……
d This celebrity's achievements include ……

11

FORTY WEEKLY UNITS

Editing tasks

Editing tasks in each week help to consolidate understanding of grammar, punctuation and spelling. Passages for editing are varied and reflect a number of different text types. Examples of how to mark up corrections are included.

Writing tasks

Writing tasks in each week help to consolidate the basic skills of written communication, from writing fluent sentences and building cohesive paragraphs to structuring responses and developing a voice. The editing passages provide a guide to the forms of writing covered in each week.

ADDITIONAL FEATURES

Vocabulary list and daily checklists

These sheets can be photocopied and are designed to help monitor progress and keep track of newly acquired words.

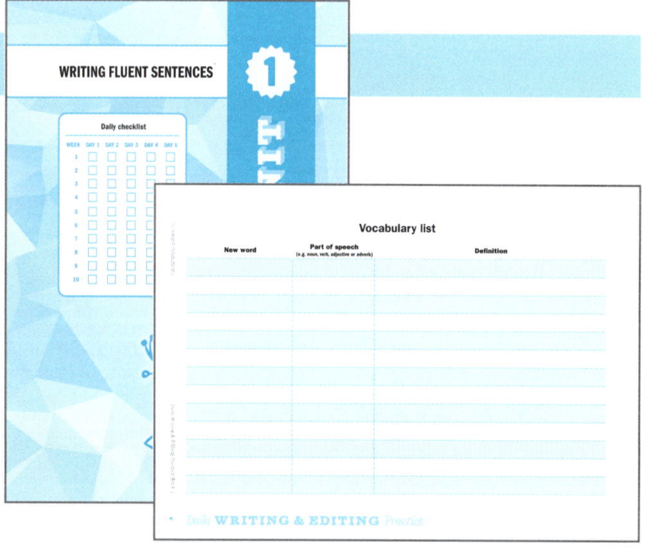

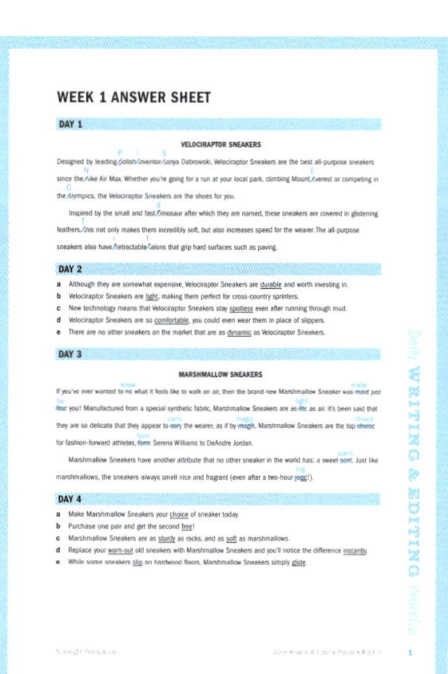
WEEK 1 ANSWER SHEET

DAY 1

VELOCIRAPTOR SNEAKERS

DAY 2

DAY 3

MARSHMALLOW SNEAKERS

DAY 4

Online answer sheets and checklists

Complete answers are provided for each day's activities. For open-ended questions, possible answers are included as a guide. Writing and editing checklists are also available and can be printed for easy access. They identify points to consider when composing and editing a piece of writing. The answer sheets and checklists are available at:
www.insightpublications.com.au/dwep

Daily WRITING & EDITING Practice

Overview

UNIT 1 WRITING FLUENT SENTENCES

WEEKS	FOCUS	TEXT TYPE
1 & 2	Choosing the right word	Advertisement
3 & 4	Forming simple and compound sentences	Profile
5 & 6	Forming complex sentences	Review
7 & 8	Varying sentence structures and lengths	Imaginative
9 & 10	Linking sentences	Informative

UNIT 2 BUILDING COHESIVE PARAGRAPHS

WEEKS	FOCUS	TEXT TYPE
11 & 12	Writing effective topic sentences	Persuasive
13 & 14	Supporting points	Informative
15 & 16	Organising information	Informative
17 & 18	Concluding statements	Informative
19 & 20	Crafting complete paragraphs	Persuasive

UNIT 3 STRUCTURING RESPONSES

WEEKS	FOCUS	TEXT TYPE
21 & 22	Deciding on a structure	Various
23 & 24	Beginning a piece (introduction/orientation)	Persuasive/Imaginative
25 & 26	Expanding ideas (evidence/complication)	Persuasive/Imaginative
27 & 28	Adding depth (persuasion/characterisation)	Persuasive/Imaginative
29 & 30	Ending a piece (conclusion/resolution)	Persuasive/Imaginative

UNIT 4 DEVELOPING A VOICE

WEEKS	FOCUS	TEXT TYPE
31 & 32	Using an informal or a formal voice	Personal/Letter
33 & 34	Writing for an audience	Various
35 & 36	Connecting with the audience	Speech
37 & 38	Writing from different points of view	Various
39 & 40	Changing voice for different purposes	Various

Vocabulary list

New word	Part of speech (e.g. noun, verb, adjective or adverb)	Definition

Marking-up guide

Use the guide below to help you mark up corrections clearly.

Correction	Example
Make capital letters	rodrigo and charlie are best friends. (marked: R, C)
Make lowercase letters	Are there Monsters under your Bed? (marked: m, b)
Add full stops	The play is selling out We should buy tickets now (marked: . .)
Add question marks	When is your birthday Is it on Sunday (marked: ? ?)
Add exclamation marks	Help Help My dog ran away. (marked: ! !)
Add commas	There are lions giraffes monkeys and tigers at the zoo. * (marked: , ,)
Add apostrophes	Lets say hello to Sarahs new friend. (marked: ' ')
Add quotation marks	Welcome to your first English class, she said. (marked: ' ')
Delete text	The parke is twenty minutes ~~minutes~~ away.
Replace text	Hilda ~~is unliking of~~ dislikes spiders and ~~intexts~~ insects.
Add text	Have ever seen full moon? (marked: you, a)
Make text italic	Their favourite films are Moana and The Lion King.

* The Oxford comma is not used in this book; the absence of one is not an example of a comma error in the editing exercises. Therefore, there should not be a comma placed before the coordinating conjunction (e.g. and, or) in a list of items.

WRITING FLUENT SENTENCES

Daily checklist

WEEK	DAY 1	DAY 2	DAY 3	DAY 4	DAY 5
1	☐	☐	☐	☐	☐
2	☐	☐	☐	☐	☐
3	☐	☐	☐	☐	☐
4	☐	☐	☐	☐	☐
5	☐	☐	☐	☐	☐
6	☐	☐	☐	☐	☐
7	☐	☐	☐	☐	☐
8	☐	☐	☐	☐	☐
9	☐	☐	☐	☐	☐
10	☐	☐	☐	☐	☐

DAY 1

Edit the advertisement below by correcting the ten capitalisation errors. The first four have been done for you.

VELOCIRAPTOR SNEAKERS

Designed by leading polish inventor sonya Dabrowski, Velociraptor Sneakers are the best all-purpose sneakers since the nike Air Max. Whether you're going for a run at your local park, climbing Mount everest or competing in the olympics, the Velociraptor Sneakers are the shoes for you.

Inspired by the small and fast Dinosaur after which they are named, these sneakers are covered in glistening feathers. this not only makes them incredibly soft, but also increases speed for the wearer. The all-purpose sneakers also have Retractable Talons that grip hard surfaces such as paving.

DAY 2

Selecting the most appropriate word for a sentence helps to communicate ideas clearly.

Fill in the gaps with the most appropriate word from the options below. The first one has been done for you.

a Although they are somewhat expensive, Velociraptor Sneakers are ___durable___ rugged / durable / resilient and worth investing in.

b Velociraptor Sneakers are ________________ light / flimsy / loose, making them perfect for cross-country sprinters.

c New technology means that Velociraptor Sneakers stay ________________ delicate / spotless / correct even after running through mud.

d Velociraptor Sneakers are so ________________ willing / easy / comfortable, you could even wear them in place of slippers.

e There are no other sneakers on the market that are as ________________ almighty / absolute / dynamic as Velociraptor Sneakers.

DAY 3

Edit the advertisement below by correcting the ten spelling errors. The first three have been done for you.

MARSHMALLOW SNEAKERS

If you've ever wanted to ~~no~~ know what it feels like to walk on air, then the brand-new Marshmallow Sneaker was ~~maid~~ made just ~~four~~ for you! Manufactured from a special synthetic fabric, Marshmallow Sneakers are as lite as air. It's been said that they are so delicate that they appear to cary the wearer, as if by magik. Marshmallow Sneakers are the top choise for fashion-forward athletes, form Serena Williams to DeAndre Jordan.

Marshmallow Sneakers have another attribute that no other sneaker in the world has: a sweet sent. Just like marshmallows, the sneakers always smell nice and fragrant (even after a two-hour jogg!).

DAY 4

Fill in the gaps using the most appropriate word from the word bank below.

glide | preference | jagged | costless | never | instantly | free

uncultured | slip | sturdy | worn-out | choice | soft | tasty

a Make Marshmallow Sneakers your ______________________ of sneaker today.

b Purchase one pair and get the second ______________________ !

c Marshmallow Sneakers are as ______________________ as rocks, and as ______________________ as marshmallows.

d Replace your ______________________ old sneakers with Marshmallow Sneakers and you'll notice the difference ______________________ .

e While some sneakers ______________________ on hardwood floors, Marshmallow Sneakers simply ______________________ .

DAY 5

❶ **Edit the advertisement below by correcting the four capitalisation errors and the four spelling errors. The first sentence has been done for you.**

ROBOT SNEAKERS

R footwear
~~r~~obot Sneakers are the future of ~~footware~~! Using the most advanced technoligy known to humankind, the designers of this game-changing sneaker have pulled out all the stops. Now you can use the autopilot function to have the sneakers move yore feet, play your music through the speakers in the laces and even levitate severel centimetres above the ground. what can't this sneaker do? other than fly you to china, the Robot Sneaker can do it all!

❷ **Fill in the gaps below to describe your favourite type of shoe.**

a Shoe type: ________________ (e.g. boot, sandal, ballet slipper)

b Material: ________________ (e.g. leather, rubber, synthetics)

c Primary purpose: ________________ (e.g. comfort, sport, fashion)

❸ **Select three words that apply to this shoe from the options below, or choose your own words.**

comfortable | inexpensive | colourful | sturdy | unique | heavy

________________ , ________________ , ________________

❹ **Using at least one of the words you selected in Question 3, explain why people should buy this shoe.**

People should buy this shoe because ________________

____

________________ .

Daily **WRITING & EDITING** Practice

DAY 1

Edit the advertisement below by correcting the seven ending punctuation errors. The first three have been done for you.

DRAGON FIRE BACKPACK

The Dragon Fire Backpack is the new craze taking schoolyards by storm? ! Is it worth the hype! ? It absolutely is, and I'm going to tell you why? . Firstly, the backpack is covered in faux dragon scales that protect your valuable possessions (like your homework) from fire? Secondly, when the zips are opened by anyone other than the owner of the backpack, an almighty roar will sound. Thirdly, each Dragon Fire Backpack comes with expandable dragon wings? Think it can't be done! Think again! The incredibly convincing wings spring out of the sides of the backpack with the push of a button. Well, what are you waiting for.

DAY 2

Using descriptive words can make sentences more interesting.

Replace the words in bold with a more descriptive option from the word bank below. The first one has been done for you.

stylish	lively	plain	whispered	exciting	specific
protects	~~exclaimed~~	neglects	unique	speechless	

'The new Dragon Fire Backpack will make you gasp,' the television presenter ___exclaimed___ **(said)**. 'It is a product like no other – it is ________________ **(uncommon)** in the truest sense of the word. No other backpack ________________ **(covers)** itself from fire and thieves, and few look as ________________ **(cool)** and trendy. While there are many ________________ **(impressive)** features of this backpack, it is the expandable dragon wings that will leave you ________________ **(silent)**. I know what my children will be getting for their birthdays this year!'

DAY 3

Edit the advertisement below by correcting the ten capitalisation errors.

INVISIBLE CRAYONS

already the number-one stationery product in the United states, Australia and Great britain, the Invisible Crayon now looks set to take over the rest of the world. Business analyst ethan lane calls the Invisible Crayon the ultimate stationery item. Unlike ordinary crayons, the Invisible Crayon makes markings that can only be seen using an Ultraviolet Light. when you write using the specially designed felt tip, your words turn invisible within seconds. Nobody can see what you've written, unless You want them to! this makes it the perfect tool for writing secret messages.

Before long, Invisible Crayons will be in every classroom and home. Get yours today, before stock runs out!

DAY 4

Replace the words in bold with a more descriptive word. The first one has been done for you.

a Invisible Crayons are ___original___ **(new)**.

b Invisible Crayons are ____________ **(cool)**.

c No other crayon has ____________ **(done)** what the Invisible Crayon has.

d Students from all over the world ____________ **(like)** the Invisible Crayon.

e Perfect for aspiring spies, the Invisible Crayon is a/an ____________ **(needed)** tool.

f Remember to ____________ **(mention)** the Invisible Crayon to all your friends!

DAY 5

1 Edit the advertisement below by correcting the four ending punctuation errors and the four capitalisation errors.

TELEPATHIC DIGITAL NOTEBOOK

Are you tired of having to write down your every thought? (i sure am?) Does your hand get tired from the weight of communicating all these thoughts! (mine sure does!) Then you need the advanced technology of the Telepathic Digital Notebook? This remarkable invention is able to read your brainwaves and transmit your thoughts straight onto the page. No Longer will you need to worry about buying hundreds of pens (and losing half of them) or about perfecting the outdated notion of clear handwriting. The Future is here?

2 Fill in the gaps below to describe a stationery item of your choice.

a Stationery item: ______________________
(e.g. pencil case, highlighter)

b Unique characteristic: ______________________
(e.g. glows in the dark, voice activation)

c Classroom use: ______________________
(e.g. writing, storage)

3 Select three words that apply to this stationery item from the options below or choose your own words.

powerful | gigantic | old-fashioned | sharp | hi-tech | compact

______________, ______________, ______________

4 Using descriptive words, explain why people should buy this item.

People should buy this item because ______________________

____

______________________.

Daily WRITING & EDITING Practice

DAY 1

Edit the profile below by correcting the ten comma errors (three in the wrong place, seven missing). The first four have been done for you. (Note that the Oxford comma is not used in this book, so no comma is needed after 'songwriter'. See p.vi for further details.)

CAMILA CABELLO

Karla Camila Cabello Estrabao known professionally as Camila Cabello is a Cuban American, singer songwriter and actress. Camila was born in Havana, Cuba, but moved to Miami Florida, with her family when she was six years old. She expressed an interest in music from an early age listening primarily to Latin artists such as Celia Cruz and Alejandro Fernández. Camila rose to prominence as a member of the girl group Fifth Harmony, which formed on *The X Factor*, (US) in 2012. They had a number of hit songs, including 'Sledgehammer' 'Work from Home' and 'Worth It' before Camila left to pursue a solo career. As a solo artist, she found success, with the number-one songs 'Havana' and 'Señorita'.

DAY 2

Fill in the gaps below to complete the simple sentences describing musical artists of your choice. Do not repeat subjects or verbs. The first one has been done for you.

> **!** Simple sentences contain a subject and a verb, and express one idea.

a ___Ariana Grande___ **(subject)** ___hits___ **(verb)** high notes in her songs.

b ______________ **(subject)** ______________ **(verb)** beautiful ballads.

c ______________ **(subject)** ______________ **(verb)** the piano.

d ______________ **(subject)** ______________ **(verb)** very catchy songs.

e ______________ **(subject)** ______________ **(verb)** complex choreography.

f ______________ **(subject)** ______________ **(verb)** crazy stunts.

g ______________ **(subject)** ______________ **(verb)** inventive costumes.

DAY 3

Edit the profile below by correcting the ten spelling errors.

NAOMI OSAKA

The daughtar of a Japanese mother and a Haitian American father, Naomi Osaka is a professional tennis player and Grand Slam champion. Osaka was borne in Japan but moved to the United States with her parents and her oldar sister Mari, who is allso a tennis player, when she was three years old. Osaka's father was enspired to teach his too children how to play tennis after seeing Venus and Serena Williams playing at the 1999 French Open.

Osaka one the US Open in 2018, becoming the first Japanese player, mail or female, to win a Grand Slam. She followed this with viktory at the 2019 Australian Open and became the first Japanese player to be ranked number won in the world.

DAY 4

Complete the simple sentences below, including as many details as possible. The first one has been done for you.

a Tennis players hit *serves, forehands, backhands, volleys and smashes* **(shots)**.

b Popular sports in my country include ______________________________ **(sports)**.

c Swimmers swim ______________________________ **(strokes)**.

d Countries in Asia include ______________________________ **(countries)**.

e Members of my family include ______________________________ **(family members)**.

DAY 5

❶ **Edit the profile below by correcting the four comma errors (two in the wrong place, two missing) and the four spelling errors.**

JESSICA MAUBOY

Jessica Mauboy is an Australian R & B and pop singer, who rose to prominence after finishing as runner-up in the forth season of *Australian Idol* in 2006. Although Mauboy was born in Darwin Northern Territory, her mother's family is from the Indigenous Kuku Yalanji tribe of Far North Queensland. Mauboy is actively involved in many organisations that help the Indigenous community, and she is ofen recognised as a positive roll model for young Indigenous girls.

Mauboy's other achiefments include, selling over 2.5 million units in Australia, having multiple number-one singles and albums representing Australia in the Eurovision Song Contest, acting and receiving numerous awards.

❷ **Fill in the gaps below to describe a celebrity of your choice.**

a Celebrity: ______________________________

b Main profession: ____________________ (e.g. actor, singer, athlete)

c Key attribute: ____________________ (e.g. funny, intelligent, hardworking)

❸ **Complete the simple sentences below to describe your chosen celebrity.**

a This celebrity lives in ______________________________.

b This celebrity is known for ______________________________

______________________________.

c This celebrity inspires ______________________________

______________________________.

d This celebrity's achievements include ______________________________

______________________________.

DAY 1

Edit the profile below by correcting the seven comma errors (five in the wrong place, two missing).

WILLIAM THE CONQUEROR

William the Conqueror was born in Normandy, (a region in modern-day France), in 1028. When his father, Duke Robert I died in 1035, William became the Duke of Normandy. As William was only eight years old at the time, Gilbert of Brionne ruled in his name (until, Gilbert was murdered three years later). William was able to maintain rule of Normandy through his alignment with powerful friends, and the power of the dukedom increased, over the next twenty years.

William would eventually lead the Norman conquest of England in 1066 defeating his rival Harold Godwinson at the Battle of Hastings. He was crowned King of England, on Christmas Day 1066 and ruled until his death in 1087.

DAY 2

Complete the compound sentences below by adding a second main clause. The first one has been done for you.

! Compound sentences contain two or more linked main clauses and help to provide additional information.

a The first states were mostly monarchies but *few countries today are ruled by a king or queen*.

b There have been many more men in power than women but ____________________.

c Many monarchies have been dismantled by revolution and ____________________.

d Monarchs today are often ceremonial heads of state but ____________________.

DAY 3

Edit the profile below by correcting the ten capitalisation errors.

SOJOURNER TRUTH

Born Isabella Baumfree, Sojourner Truth was an african American abolitionist and women's rights activist in nineteenth-century america. She was born into slavery in the state of New York in 1797. throughout the first twenty years of her life she was bought and sold four times, and endured harsh physical treatment by her Owners. Baumfree escaped to freedom with her infant daughter in 1826. She converted to christianity and renamed herself Sojourner Truth, believing that a spirit called her to preach the Truth.

After gaining her freedom, Truth devoted much of her life to the Abolition of Slavery. She used her growing reputation in this field to help recruit black troops for the Union Army, and her work led her to meet President abraham lincoln in 1864.

DAY 4

Complete the compound sentences by adding one of the clauses from the box below.

- they bought her freedom for twenty dollars
- she dictated her recollections to a friend who helped to publish her memoirs
- she sued for his return and won her case

a Sojourner Truth could not read or write, so ______________________________

______________________________.

b Sojourner Truth's five-year-old son was illegally sold into slavery, so ______________________________

______________________________.

c Sojourner Truth stayed with a nearby abolitionist family after fleeing, and ______________________________

______________________________.

Daily **WRITING & EDITING** *Practice*

DAY 5

❶ **Edit the profile below by correcting the four comma errors (three in the wrong place, one missing) and the four capitalisation errors.**

MAE JEMISON

Over the course of her life, Mae Jemison has been a doctor an engineer and a teacher, but she is perhaps best known as the first African American woman to travel in Space. She was born in Alabama in 1956 and displayed a love of science, from an early age. She obtained several Degrees at a number of prestigious Universities, in the United States before working as a general practitioner.

Pursuing her childhood dream, Jemison applied to NASA's astronaut program in 1987. five years later she joined six other astronauts on the space shuttle *Endeavour*, which completed 126 orbits, around the world.

❷ **Fill in the gaps below to describe a historical figure of your choice.**

a Historical figure: ______________________ (e.g. Marie Curie, Ned Kelly)

b Area of speciality: ______________________ (e.g. science, leadership)

c Key attribute: ______________________ (e.g. intelligence, humour)

❸ **Complete the compound sentences below to describe your chosen historical figure.**

a This historical figure achieved incredible things while alive, and helped to

____.

b This historical figure faced obstacles such as ______________________

______________________, but overcame this ______________________

____.

❹ **Explain why this historical figure is still remembered today.**

____

____.

DAY 1

Edit the film review below by correcting the five ending punctuation errors.

A THOUSAND STARS

A Thousand Stars is a drama directed by Lindsay Maxwell that will appeal to viewers of a wide range of ages, The film follows the story of brothers Jake and Josh; Fascinated by their uncle's collection of science-fiction movies, the boys dream of escaping their small town and exploring outer space, However, first they must find a way to get there! Not to be put off by their lack of expertise, the brothers decide to build their own rocket ship – with hilarious results?

A tender portrait of childhood and a tribute to the power of imagination, this film will make you both laugh and cry, I'm giving it one thousand stars out of five!

DAY 2

Fill in the gaps with a main clause of your own creation to complete the complex sentences below. The first one has been done for you.

! Complex sentences consist of a main clause and a subordinate clause that gives more information.

a When people watch *A Thousand Stars*, *they will be amazed by the special effects*.

b If you only see one film this year, __________.

c __________ after you see *A Thousand Stars*.

d Even though Jake is the older brother, __________.

e Because *A Thousand Stars* appeals to a wide range of ages, __________.

Daily **WRITING & EDITING** *Practice*

DAY 3

Edit the film review below by correcting the eight spelling errors.

VOLCANO HUNTER

A documentary film directed by Charles Carrasco, *Volcano Hunter* is a thriling experiense with enough reel-life action to keep viewers watching till the end. Carrasco's debut film takes us into the world of mysterious Tom Lanyon, a profeshional 'volcano hunter' who spends his time filming and exploring activ volcanoes. With the best of his carear behind him, Lanyon decides to embark on one last adventure before he retyres. A nail-biting insight into the life of a real modern-day explorer, *Volcano Hunter* is not your averadge boring documentary. The stunning visual depictions of exploding volcanoes alone will leave you gasping for air. Four and a half stars out of five.

DAY 4

Fill in the gaps to complete the subordinate clause in the complex sentences below. The first one has been done for you.

a Before *you watch Volcano Hunter*, do some preliminary research about volcanoes.

b Just like ______________________________, this film is full of fire.

c If ______________________________,
then you'll love *Volcano Hunter*.

d While ______________________________
______________________________, you will enjoy *this* documentary.

e Although ______________________________
______________________________, the film is still easy to understand.

DAY 5

❶ **Edit the film review below by correcting the four ending punctuation errors and the four spelling errors.**

THE DALMATIAN CONUNDRUM

Svetlana Milic's newest film, *The Dalmatian Conundrum*, is an enjoyible twist on the mystery genre that will keep the audience guessing – When the mayor's prized Dalmatian goes missing, privat detektive Morgan Reed is called in to solve the mystery and recover the pooch, Things aren't as they seem in this small town, however, and Reed soon discovers that many people wood prefer she let sleeping dogs lie – including the mayor himself? Fans of Agatha Christie will delight in this new crime movie Four stars out of five.

❷ **Fill in the gaps below to describe a film of your choice.**

a Film title: ______________________________

b Director: ______________________________

c Genre: ______________________________ (e.g. thriller, fantasy, musical)

d Your rating: ______________ out of five stars

❸ **Complete the complex sentences below to describe your chosen film.**

a Although the narrative begins ______________________________,

______________________________.

b Even though the characters ______________________________,

______________________________.

❹ **Explain why people should or should not see this film.**

____

______________________________.

DAY 1

Edit the book review below by correcting the eight capitalisation errors.

KILIMANJARO BLUES

Kilimanjaro Blues is a heart-wrenching Young Adult novel written by Ella mae Nnadi. The story follows the journey of Bobby, an antisocial blind fifteen-year-old who dreams of becoming the first blind person to climb mount Kilimanjaro. The book details the struggles he must overcome, from finding his way to the Kilimanjaro National Park in Tanzania to convincing his widowed father to believe in him.

nnadi is an Expert Storyteller who is able to draw a portrait of a complex character. Despite the character's flaws, we feel empathy for him and want him to succeed. Five stars out of Five!

DAY 2

Fill in the gaps to complete the embedded clauses in the complex sentences below, using your own ideas. The first one has been done for you.

An embedded clause (a type of subordinate clause) 'interrupts' a main clause to give more information.

a Ella Mae Nnadi, who *worked as a psychologist for twelve years*, creates fascinating and multifaceted characters.

b Tanzania, where ______________________________, is described in vivid detail.

c Bobby's father, who ______________________________ ______________________________, helps to reveal the difficulties of raising a blind child.

d The use of the first person (that is, using personal pronouns such as 'I' and 'me'), which ______________________________ ______________________________, allows the reader to better understand the main character.

DAY 3

Edit the book review below by correcting the eight comma errors (four in the wrong place, four missing).

HOW TO PROTECT THE EARTH

How to Protect the Earth is a nonfiction book written by well-known, sustainability activist Liliana Jenkins. The book which is based on years of research conducted by Jenkins gives readers simple steps to follow, that will help to save the planet. These include using public transport to limit carbon emissions recycling taking shorter showers in summer and planting trees.

While the message of the book is positive, Jenkins' writing style is, at times, boring and repetitive. The inclusion of images, and graphs, helps to add variety and colour to the text, and overall the book succeeds in getting its message across. Three and a half stars out of five.

DAY 4

Complete the complex sentences by adding one of the clauses from the box below.

which contains helpful and achievable tips
which inform readers about the real world
which include founding a recycling plant

a Nonfiction books, ______________________________

______________________, are sometimes just as exciting as fiction books.

b Liliana Jenkins' career achievements, ______________________________

______________________, have helped her to write this book.

c *How to Protect the Earth*, ______________________________

______________________, is that rare book that can inspire change.

DAY 5

1 Edit the book review below by correcting the four capitalisation errors and the four comma errors (one in the wrong place, three missing).

MAGES VS MERMAIDS

Set in a fictional world, where magical creatures battle one another for supremacy, *Mages vs Mermaids* is a thrilling fantasy novel by scottish writer Woodrow Zverev. The book follows Merman 854 a disgruntled former member of the ruling mermaid family, who betrays his people to help the mages ascend to the throne. But there are other forces at work, too. The werewolves and centaurs have formed an unlikely alliance and are threatening to destroy everything and everyone. A fascinating tale of loyalty treachery and ambition *mages vs mermaids* will keep you up all night. five stars out of five.

2 Fill in the gaps below to describe a book of your choice.

a Book title: ______________________________

b Author: ______________________________

c Genre: ______________________ (e.g. mystery, science fiction, humour)

d Rating: __________ out of five stars

3 Complete the complex sentences below to describe your chosen book.

a The main character, who ______________________________,

______________________________.

b The climax of the book, which ______________________________,

______________________________.

4 Explain why people should or should not read this book.

____

______________________________.

Daily WRITING & EDITING Practice

DAY 1

Edit the imaginative piece below by correcting the eight spelling errors.

IN THE FOREST

Abdullah was runing as fast as his legs could carry him. He stumbeld over vines and shrubs, but kept pushing forward, desperate to find his sister.

'Padma!' he screamed into the void. 'Padma!'

As he made his way further and further into the thic undergrowth, the rays of sunshine that had filled him with confidance began to disappear. All that was left was an eerie darkness that extended as far as the eye could see. Using the trunks of trees to guide his steep, Abdullah shufled slowly forward. He kept screaming out his sister's name, hoping that she would here him, when suddenly the sound of a wolf howling punctured the silense of the forest.

DAY 2

Fill in the gaps using the most appropriate sentence opener from the word bank below.

! Using different openings for sentences helps to add variety and interest.

All of a sudden	Hesitantly	Without a doubt	Unbelievably	As time went by

Padma hugged herself tightly. ______________________, this was the most scared she had ever felt. Fumbling with her shoelaces in the darkness of the cave, she tried to distract herself. But all she could think about was how hungry she was. ______________________, her hunger had become unbearable.

______________________ she got up. She couldn't stand it any longer; she needed to get out of there! ______________________, she stepped out of the cave, looking out into the darkness of the forest for the first time in days. What she saw filled her with horror. ______________________, it was her brother Abdullah, and he was surrounded by a pack of snarling wolves.

DAY 3

Edit the imaginative piece below by correcting the nine apostrophe errors (two in the wrong place, seven missing). The first four have been done for you.

CAT AND MOUSE

Im motoring down the freeway, swerving between trucks and car's with total abandon. Theres a police car right on my tail! Kensington Avenues just a few minutes away. If I can get there quickly enough I can go through the secret underground tunnel and lose them. Its the perfect plan. It cant fail!

I drive as fast as my little Honda Civic can go. When there's just enough distance between me and the police car I veer into Kensington Avenue, primed to escape as Ive done so many times before. Thats when I see them. A line of police cars' waiting just for me …

DAY 4

Rewrite the sentences below so that they do not begin with a pronoun. The first two have been done for you.

a I look around my prison cell for a way to escape.

Looking around my prison cell, I search for a way to escape.

b He spoke to the other prisoners and learned that the guards were very vigilant.

By speaking to the other prisoners, he learned that the guards were very vigilant.

c I sit silently and fumble with my shoelaces. ______

______

d He thinks about his family and begins to cry. ______

______

e He tries to forget where he is and goes to sleep. ______

______

DAY 5

❶ **Edit the imaginative piece below by correcting the five spelling errors and the five apostrophe errors (one in the wrong place, four missing).**

DETECTIVE MEURSAULT

Its the dead of nite when Detective Meursault arrives at the seen of the crime. He walk's into the locked-down shopping centre and sees three people gathered around a dead body. Theres the security gard who called him, a woman with a dog and a moody-looking teenager.

The detective begins as he always does, looking around for any evidence that could point to the killer, but theres nothing out of the ordinery. This is going to be a trickey one, he thinks to himself.

'Everyone in this room is a suspect,' he says loudly, with menace in his voice. 'Were not leaving here until I discover who committed this murder.'

❷ **Read the sentence openers below and use them to write a short imaginative scene in the first person.**

The creature is still following me. Running as fast as I can, I ______________________

____.

I think I'm safe, at least for now. But ______________________________

____.

Using all my force, I jump. I look back and ___________________________

____.

There's only one way for me to get out of here alive! Tossing aside my backpack, I

____

____.

Daily WRITING & EDITING Practice

DAY 1

Edit the imaginative piece below by correcting the five ending punctuation errors.

TORPEDO TANYA

Tanya steeled herself Out in the distance, the villainous Wicked Moon Princess was speeding across the wide expanse of water in her high-powered jet boat. If Tanya didn't act fast, the Wicked Moon Princess would escape? Not only would she escape, but she would get away with the weapons of mass destruction. Tanya closed her eyes, took one giant leap and crashed into the icy water below, As soon as she felt the water surrounding her, Tanya's shark-like instincts kicked into gear and her eyes narrowed, focusing on her prey. She began swimming, her legs slowly morphing into fins and scales? Now she was rocketing towards the Wicked Moon Princess at a tremendous speed ... she wasn't getting away this time

DAY 2

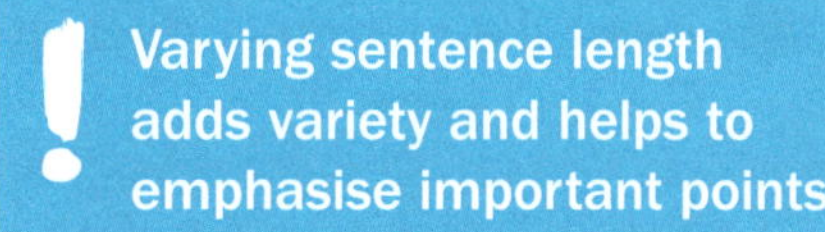

Rewrite the numbered bold sentences below as short sentences. The first one has been done for you.

The Wicked Moon Princess felt the water beneath her rumble and groan. **(1) Her nemesis, Torpedo Tanya, had travelled quickly to arrive here, now, under her jet boat.** She was going to disrupt her plans for world domination once again. But the Wicked Moon Princess wasn't going to let that happen. **(2) There was a secret plan that she had thought about for some time that she was sure would stop her shapeshifting nemesis.** Beneath her jet boat was a cage holding a ferocious, bloodthirsty shark who would end this once and for all.

(3) 'Open the hatch using your special tools so that the shark can swim out of the cage,' she ordered one of her underlings.

1 *Torpedo Tanya was here!*

2 ______________________________

3 ______________________________

DAY 3

Edit the imaginative piece below by correcting the ten quotation mark errors (three in the wrong place, seven missing). The first three have been done for you.

INTO THE VAMPIRE CAVE

'Listen up, everybody,' the commander yelled above the din. 'Tomorrow morning we begin our expedition to find our lost brother.'

The commander looked out at the soldiers assembled before him. They stood 'proud and tall', as they always did. But where there would usually be determination and resolve in their eyes, there was only fear.

I won't lie, he said. This will be our most difficult mission yet. Our brother was last seen in the Vampire Cave. We don't know what he was doing in this forbidden place, 'but it is clear that the terrible creatures who live there have taken him prisoner. We must be ready to defeat these creatures in order to save our brother!

DAY 4

Place the sentences in a logical order.

- Venturing further into the cave, they began to see objects that belonged to their friend.
- 'There he is!' they screamed, horrified at the pale man in the cage.
- The soldiers crept into the dark cave.
- The soldiers pushed on, ignoring the pain.
- As soon as they entered, a cloud of bats flew towards them and began biting them.

DAY 5

1 Edit the imaginative piece below by correcting the five ending punctuation errors and the five quotation mark errors (one in the wrong place, four missing).

THE END

'Wake up, wake up?' Dad was standing above me, shaking me vigorously.'

What are you doing, I stammered.

'You were having another nightmare,' he replied, a worried look on his face

I realised that I was drenched in sweat. It had happened again. One of those terrible nightmares. No, not a nightmare, a vision, The things I was seeing in my dreams were coming true.

'It was terrible, I whispered, tears streaming down my face, The police were taking you away from me again.'

2 Write a short imaginative scene using one of the starting sentences below. Remember to vary your sentence openers and the lengths of your sentences.

- The storm outside was monstrous.
- I found myself at a fork in the road.
- 'What have you done?'

____

____

____

____

____

____

____

____

____

DAY 1

Edit the informative piece below by correcting the eight capitalisation errors.

LET'S VISIT SRI LANKA

Located in the south of asia, Sri Lanka is known as 'the Pearl of the indian ocean'. With a year-round tropical climate, pristine sandy beaches and delicious food, Sri Lanka is the perfect travel destination. Must-Dos include tasting an authentic lentil and chicken curry and marvelling at the buddhist-inspired Temple of the Tooth.

Other highlights include the town of Nuwara Eliya, which is referred to as 'little England' because of its colonial-era buildings and Tudor-style Hotels, and the Minneriya National Park. during the Sri Lankan dry season, hundreds of Elephants gather at this site to feed, socialise and frolic in the water.

DAY 2

Sort the transition words below into the correct categories, then fill in the gaps in the sentences using an appropriate transition word.

! Transition words and phrases help to connect ideas and make sentences read smoothly.

as a result | also | even though | despite | moreover
for this reason | on the other hand | therefore | furthermore

Addition	Contrast	Cause/effect

a The most popular sport in Sri Lanka is cricket. Rugby union, volleyball and athletics are ______________________ very popular.

b Sri Lanka has a very warm climate. ______________________ beaches are a popular tourist attraction.

DAY 3

Edit the informative piece below by correcting the eight comma errors (two in the wrong place, six missing).

LET'S VISIT JORDAN

The Middle Eastern country of Jordan is known not only as the land of lost cities and epic adventures, but also as a site of natural beauty. There are many historical sites, in Jordan the best-known of which is the archaeological city of Petra. Located in the south of the country Petra is estimated to have existed for more than 9000 years.

The capital city of Amman with its many Greek and Roman ruins is another highlight of Jordan. It is a centre for the arts, with many exhibitions from Iraqi Syrian Palestinian and Jordanian artists. This makes it the perfect place to go, and experience some authentic Middle Eastern culture.

DAY 4

Rewrite the sentences below and include an appropriate transition word or phrase. The first one has been done for you.

a The Dana Biosphere Reserve in Jordan is home to many plants and animals. It is one of the best places to stargaze at night.

The Dana Biosphere Reserve in Jordan is home to many plants and animals.

It is ***also*** *one of the best places to stargaze at night.*

b Jordan is surrounded by warring countries. Jordan is a safe place to travel.

____

____

c There are many archaeological sites in Jordan. History fans will love visiting this country.

____

____

DAY 5

❶ **Edit the informative piece below by correcting the five capitalisation errors and the five comma errors (two in the wrong place, three missing).**

LET'S VISIT SERBIA

the Balkan nation of Serbia is full of attractions, that will appeal to both adrenaline seekers and those looking for a relaxing break. Notably, Serbia's Capital, Belgrade, is sure to charm. With music art history parks and lakes, the city is full of wonder; however, Belgrade is perhaps best known for its wild nightlife. There are party boats all along the sava and danube rivers, and a diverse mix of bars and clubs.

Serbia is also home to many monasteries. These stately buildings are calm places of worship and are perfect, for viewing Frescoes (mural paintings) and enjoying Serbia's softer side.

❷ **Fill in the gaps below to describe a country of your choice.**

a Country: ______________________________

b Capital city: ______________________________

❸ **Using the transition words and phrases below as a guide, explain why people should visit this country.**

The country of ____________________ is an amazing place to visit.

Firstly, there are lots of ______________________________

______________________________ .

In addition, ______________________________

______________________________ .

Even though ______________________________ ,

______________________________ .

On the whole, this country ______________________________

______________________________ .

DAY 1

Edit the informative piece below by correcting the eight spelling errors.

ALL ABOUT ULURU

Uluru is one of the greatast natral wonders of the world. It is located in Australia, in the Northern Territory's 'Red Centre', and is thought to have been formed more than 550 million years ago. Hundreads of thousands of tourists visit the landmarc every year.

While it is a tourist attraction two many people, Uluru is also considered a deepley spiritual and sakred place to Indigenous Australians. To the Aṉangu people of central Australia, Uluru holds a special cultural significance: they believe that it was created at the beginning of time bi their ancestral spirits.

DAY 2

! Linking sentences together helps readers to progress from one idea to the next.

Fill in the gaps below with an appropriate transition word or phrase from the word bank below.

In addition	Also	For this reason	Although
For example	On the other hand	However	

There are a number of Indigenous landmarks in Australia. ______________________ Uluru is the best-known of these, each landmark is unique in its own way. ______________ ______________ the Grampians in Victoria is home to rare Aboriginal rock art paintings. ______________________ there are hiking trails, wildflower displays and many other natural wonders. ______________________ the Grampians National Park, which is part of the Gariwerd Aboriginal cultural landscape, is one of Australia's most recognisable nature reserves.

DAY 3

Edit the informative piece below by correcting the eight apostrophe errors (three in the wrong place, five missing).

ALL ABOUT THE TAJ MAHAL

Indias Taj Mahal is a mausoleum (a building that houses' tombs) located in the city of Agra. Shah Jahan, ruler of the Mughal Empire (covering modern-day' India, Pakistan, Afghanistan and Bangladesh), ordered the mausoleums construction to house the tomb of his deceased wife, Mumtaz Mahal.

It isnt hard to see why this landmarks so popular. The main building was built between 1631 and 1653 using white marble, and its exterior design incorporates Islamic, Iranian, Persian and Indian style's. However, thats not all there is to the Taj Mahal. In addition to the mausoleum, it has an inner courtyard, a mosque and gardens.

DAY 4

Fill in the gaps to complete the linked sentences below. The first one has been done for you.

a Landmarks often represent the cultural heritage of a country. In addition, *they bring tourists into the country and help the economy*.

b Even though there are many well-known landmarks, ____________________________________.

c Some notable landmarks, such as the Sydney Opera House and Burj Khalifa, were built by people, but ____________________________________.

d Landmarks provide a point of reference for tourists who are unfamiliar with the city. For this reason ____________________________________.

Daily WRITING & EDITING Practice

DAY 5

1 Edit the informative piece below by correcting the four spelling errors and the four apostrophe errors (one in the wrong place, three missing).

ALL ABOUT VICTORIA FALLS

Its official: Victoria Falls is travel enthusiasts next big thing! Found on the Zambezi River, at the bordor between Zambia and Zimbabwe, this natural wonder is approximately twice as wide and twice as deep as Niagara Falls.

At the hight of the rainy season, theres more than five hundred million cubic metres of water per minute falling over the edge. Colums of spray and mist from the waterfall can be scene from far away, which led the Kalolo-Lozi people to name the falls' Mosi-oa-Tunya ('The Smoke That Thunders') in the 1800s.

2 Fill in the gaps below to describe a landmark of your choice.

a Landmark: ____________________

b Location: ____________________

3 Using transition words and phrases, explain what makes this landmark unique or special.

To begin with, ____________________

____

____

____

____

____

____

____

____________________.

BUILDING COHESIVE PARAGRAPHS

Daily checklist

WEEK	DAY 1	DAY 2	DAY 3	DAY 4	DAY 5
11	☐	☐	☐	☐	☐
12	☐	☐	☐	☐	☐
13	☐	☐	☐	☐	☐
14	☐	☐	☐	☐	☐
15	☐	☐	☐	☐	☐
16	☐	☐	☐	☐	☐
17	☐	☐	☐	☐	☐
18	☐	☐	☐	☐	☐
19	☐	☐	☐	☐	☐
20	☐	☐	☐	☐	☐

DAY 1

Edit the persuasive piece below by correcting the nine spelling errors.

THE IMPORTANCE OF HOMEWORK

Doing schoolwork at home is a valuable part of the lerning process. It gives students the oportunity to practise what they have learnt in class and consolidate their knowlege. At home, students can reveiw the content of a lesson away from the distraktions of the schoolyard and practise the things they might find difficult.

Homework is also an importent tool for teachers and parents. Reviewing homework gives teachers a good indication of a student's progres. For parents, homework is an opportunity to get involved with their child's learning by ansering their questions or lending asistance.

DAY 2

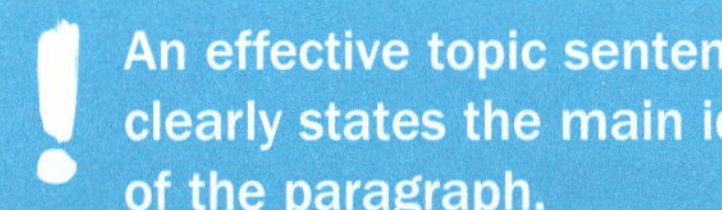

An effective topic sentence clearly states the main idea of the paragraph.

Highlight the topic sentence in each of the paragraphs below and rewrite the sentence to make it more specific. The first one has been done for you.

a Reading helps students. Regular reading can improve the ability to communicate, write and memorise information. These are all key skills that can help students succeed.

More specific topic sentence: *Reading helps students develop important skills.*

b Reading is beneficial. Some studies suggest that reading can reduce stress. It has also been shown to be more effective than other relaxation methods.

More specific topic sentence: ______________________

____

c Reading books is good. When you read a book, all of your attention is focused on the story. This helps to avoid distractions.

More specific topic sentence: ______________________

____

Daily WRITING & EDITING Practice

DAY 3

Edit the persuasive piece below by correcting the eight comma errors (four in the wrong place, four missing).

WHY STUDY A FOREIGN LANGUAGE?

Studying a foreign language can, significantly improve brain function. Research shows that children who learn a foreign language are better at multi-tasking problem-solving and creative thinking. They also perform better than their classmates in subjects like maths science and, even English, and are less likely to suffer dementia in old age.

Speaking a foreign language broadens a student's career options. Having another language under your belt means you can take advantage of opportunities to live study and work overseas. Many multinational companies favour candidates who can speak another language over those who, can't for example. Bilingual workers have also been shown to earn higher salaries, than their monolingual colleagues.

DAY 4

Reorder the sentences below, beginning with the topic sentence, to form a paragraph.

- Students who play team sports are more easily able to make friends.
- Exercising regularly improves both physical and mental health.
- Playing team sports has a range of health benefits.
- Team sports also encourage regular exercise.
- This is important, as social contact reduces the likelihood of depression.

DAY 5

❶ **Edit the persuasive piece below by correcting the five spelling errors and the five comma errors (two in the wrong place, three missing).**

IT'S TIME TO BAN THE SCHOOL UNIFORM

Being forced to wear a school uniform prevents students from expressing themselves. Clothing is a major part of students' identity. It allows them to share how they feel about certin issues, that they may not be abel to express in words. By not alowing students to do this schools are restricting the development of children's personalities.

The cost of uniforms can bee very high, for some parents. Sending a child to school five days a weak means at least two or three outfits, as well as a hat a backpack and a special pair of shoes. Paying for these on top of the cost of textbooks stationery and school fees can quickly add up.

❷ **Using the example above as a guide, write two distinct topic sentences on a school issue of your choice.**

Issue: ______________________________

(e.g. length of school holidays, healthy food options in the canteen)

Position on the issue: ______________________________

Topic sentence about how the issue affects students: ______________________________

____

______________________________.

Topic sentence about how the issue affects parents: ______________________________

____

______________________________.

Daily WRITING & EDITING Practice

DAY 1

Edit the persuasive piece below by correcting the five ending punctuation errors.

FLYING CARS: THE FUTURE OF TRANSPORTATION?

Electric flying cars can help us reduce traffic and air pollution.. As our cities grow, so does the number of cars on the roads, This has led to traffic congestion as well as an increase in the level of air pollution. As flying cars became more popular, fewer people would drive, leaving our roads less congested and our air less polluted –

The flying car is also very efficient, For one, flying in a direct line, rather than following roads, can get you to your destination more quickly? Research shows that, on average, an electric flying car with four people inside produces almost half the greenhouse gas emissions of a car with a conventional engine.

DAY 2

Sentences in a paragraph must relate back to the topic sentence of that paragraph.

Write a topic sentence for each paragraph that clearly states the main idea.

THE BENEFITS OF E-BIKES

a Topic sentence: ______________________________

____

E-bikes cost a fraction of the price of buying a car or a motorbike, for example. Powered by battery instead of petrol, they are also much cheaper to run and require a lot less maintenance than a combustion-engine vehicle.

b Topic sentence: ______________________________

____

The average bicycle commuter travels at a speed of around fifteen kilometres per hour. An e-bike, on the other hand, can travel up to twenty-five kilometres per hour. You can get to your destination much faster!

DAY 3

Edit the persuasive piece below by correcting the seven apostrophe errors (three in the wrong place, four missing).

VIRTUAL: THE REALITY OF THE FUTURE

Virtual reality allows you to see and do things you simply cant in real life. Perhaps you've always wanted to visit Tokyo, Japan? Or maybe youd like to know what it feels like to be a billionaires son or daughter for a couple of hours? Virtual reality gives you the chance to do all of these – and from the comfort of your own home.

More than just entertainment, however, virtual reality can also be a powerful educational tool. Its particularly useful for people who work in dangerous environments. Police officer's, soldier's and firefighter's, for example, can use virtual reality to practise their skills in a simulated situation.

DAY 4

Choose the most effective topic sentence for the paragraph below and explain why you chose this option.

Architects use virtual reality for their projects.

Virtual reality can save organisations time and money.

Virtual reality is sometimes abbreviated as VR.

Topic sentence: ______________________________

____

Virtual reality gives workers the ability to complete projects from remote locations. This reduces travel time and its associated costs. For example, architects can study buildings from the other side of the world without having to fly to another country.

Explanation: ______________________________

____

DAY 5

1 Edit the persuasive piece below by correcting the four ending punctuation errors and the four apostrophe errors (one in the wrong place, three missing).

MUSIC STREAMING SERVICES

THE GOOD: Music streaming services make music easier to access ... Spotifys premium service, for example, gives customers' the ability to listen to music on multiple devices from anywhere in the world. Streaming services also offer a wide selection of music catering to a variety of tastes –

THE BAD: While streaming companies make good profits from their subscription services, its a different story for most musicians, Unless youre a famous artist, earning a decent amount of money through streaming services is difficult? The average Australian musician earns just 0.7 cents per song streamed!

2 Using the example above as a guide, write two topic sentences on an issue of your choice.

Issue: ____________________

(e.g. mobile phone use in the classroom)

a THE GOOD:

Topic sentence: ____________________

____

____

b THE BAD:

Topic sentence: ____________________

____

____

Daily WRITING & EDITING Practice

DAY 1

Edit the informative piece below by correcting the eight comma errors (two in the wrong place, six missing).

THE SUPER SOAKER

Like many inventions the Super Soaker was the result of an accident. The original version was invented in 1982, by Lonnie Johnson an inventor and engineer from Alabama. Johnson was trying to build a heat pump a device that mechanically transfers heat to another source when the pump began to shoot water across the room. Applying the same idea Johnson built a model of a water pistol using glass a pipe and a soft-drink bottle. His invention was purchased by a toy company in 1990 and went on to become one of the top-selling toys, in the world.

DAY 2

Supporting sentences give more information about the topic.

Reorder the supporting sentences below to complete the paragraph. The topic sentence has been done for you.

- Today, more than 250 million Slinkys have been sold around the world.
- James had been working on a device to secure equipment to ships in rough seas when he accidentally knocked over a coiled spring.
- The Slinky was invented by naval engineer Richard James in 1943.
- Watching the spring move in a series of arcs, he decided it would make a good toy.

THE SLINKY

While most people know what a Slinky is, not many know the story behind it. ______________

____

____

____

____

____

Daily WRITING & EDITING Practice

DAY 3

Edit the informative piece below by correcting the nine spelling errors.

THE TREADMILL

Contrary to what you might think, the treadmil is not a resent invention. It was originaly created in 1818 by Englishmen Sir William Cubitt as a form of punishment for prisoners. Convicts would spend hours stepping on the spokes of a giant paddlewheel, which was used to pump water or power mills. Cubitt's invention spread through the prison system in Englind and was even exported to America. But use of the early treadmill also led to a high number of injurys among prisoners, and the practice was finally banned in 1898 for being excesively cruel. It wasn't until the 1970s that the moden treadmill would apear – this time, however, as a tool for exercise, rather than labour.

DAY 4

Read the passage below and draw a line through the three sentences that do not support the topic sentence.

THE BAND-AID

The invention of the Band-Aid is a great example of the power of a simple idea. Ideas can be either simple or complex. The original concept was developed in 1920 by Earle Dickson, an employee at the American pharmaceutical company Johnson & Johnson. Johnson & Johnson was founded in 1886. Dickson's wife would often cut or burn herself while cooking, and dressing her wounds was time-consuming. To save time, Dickson created a series of ready-made bandages by placing squares of cotton gauze along a strip of tape, which could then be quickly cut and applied to a wound. Dickson lived in New Jersey, United States, for most of his life. Today, the name Band-Aid is known throughout America and Australia, with more than 1 billion sold worldwide.

DAY 5

❶ **Edit the informative piece below by correcting the five comma errors (five missing) and the five spelling errors.**

MONOPOLY

Monopoly is based on an originel idea by Elizabeth Magie a writer actor and part-time game designer. Magie's version entitled The Landlord's Game was intended to show how one person owning all the land was a bad thing. It had two sets of rules: one in which players tried to bankrupd their competitors and another in which players shared the wealth they made from acquiring property. After coming across her game, Philadelphia man Charles Darrow dropped the second set of rules and repackaged it as Monopoly. He eventualy sold his versin to Parker Brothers becoming the first millionair game designer in history. Magie, however, received just $500 from the company for her idea.

❷ **Write three questions for the topic sentence below to develop ideas for supporting points. The first one has been done for you.**

Topic sentence: Monopoly is a popular board game invented in the twentieth century.

a Question 1: *Who invented it?*

b Question 2: ______________________

c Question 3: ______________________

❸ **Fill in the gaps to develop ideas for supporting points for an invention of your choice.**

Invention: ______________________ (e.g. iPad, PlayStation)

Topic sentence: ______________________

a Question 1: ______________________

b Question 2: ______________________

c Question 3: ______________________

DAY 1

Edit the informative piece below by correcting the six capitalisation errors.

THE DISCOVERY OF CORNFLAKES

today, cornflakes are one of the best-known breakfast cereals in the World, but if it wasn't for a happy accident we might not have had them to enjoy every morning. At the end of the nineteenth century, dr John Harvey Kellogg and his brother Will keith Kellogg made a game-changing discovery. One day, the brothers accidentally left some boiled wheat sitting out in a field. the wheat went stale, but rather than throwing it away they tried to roll it into dough. They got flakes instead, and once the flakes were toasted they knew they had Something delicious on their hands. The brothers experimented with other grains, including corn, and that is how cornflakes came to be.

DAY 2

Write two questions for supporting ideas for each of the topics below. The first one has been done for you.

> Strong supporting sentences answer the reader's questions about the topic.

a Discovery 1 *How was it discovered?* 2 *Who discovered it?*

b World record 1 ______

2 ______

c Recipe 1 ______

2 ______

d Film review 1 ______

2 ______

e Crime report 1 ______

2 ______

DAY 3

Edit the informative piece below by correcting the six apostrophe errors (two in the wrong place, four missing).

PROXIMA CENTAURI b

Proxima Centauri b, a planet in the Alpha Centauri system, was discovered by scientists in 2016. Estimated to be 1.3 times the mass of Earth, the planet takes 11.2 days to circle it's star. The planets star is highly unpredictable and emits harmful amounts of radiation. Scientist's are still trying to determine whether Proxima Centauri b is a planet that could support human life one day. If there's one thing we know, however, its that humans wont be visiting that part of the galaxy anytime soon. Proxima Centauri b is located approximately 4.2 light-years (40 trillion kilometres) from Earth – a long trip in anyones book.

DAY 4

In each of the options below, identify which is the topic sentence (TS) and which is the supporting sentence (SS), then explain your decision.

a Percy Spencer realised that the microwave beams used for radar systems could warm up food when a chocolate bar in his pocket melted as a result of the beam. TS SS

The invention of the microwave oven is an interesting story. TS SS

Explanation: ______________________________

____

b The colour mauve was an accidental discovery by William Perkin. TS SS

Perkin had been researching a cure for the deadly disease malaria when he discovered a new colour instead. TS SS

Explanation: ______________________________

____

DAY 5

1 Edit the informative piece below by correcting the three capitalisation errors and the three apostrophe errors (two in the wrong place, one missing).

OBSESSED WITH OBSESSION

calvin Klein's Obsession is one of the most popular perfumes among humans, but apparently its also a hit with big cats. This discovery was made in 1998 when a zookeeper from Dallas, texas, sprayed the perfume into an Enclosure holding wild cats. She found that the cats spent a lot more time sniffing the perfume than other smells. The reason for this is simple, if a little strange. Obsession perfume contains a chemical compound made from the scent produced by civets (small nocturnal mammals' similar to weasels and raccoons). The smell of the perfume makes cat's curious and they want to overpower the scent with their own.

2 Select a discovery and write four supporting ideas to form an outline of a paragraph. The first supporting point has been done for you.

Discovery: ______________________________

(e.g. a planet, a cure for a disease, a chemical element)

Supporting point 1: *This sentence will give details of the person who made the discovery.*

Supporting point 2: ______________________________

______________________________.

Supporting point 3: ______________________________

______________________________.

Supporting point 4: ______________________________

______________________________.

DAY 1

Edit the informative piece below by correcting the six spelling errors.

THE CLEVER COYOTE

When it comes to exploration, the coyote would give any explorer in history a run for their money. Originally native to two-thirds of the United States and a small area of Mexico, this tuff canine can now be found in every state except Hawaii. The coyote's rise is due to a number of facters. These include its ability to adapt to different climates and landscapes, and the decline of the wolf – the coyote's natural enemie. However, it's not just rural areas were coyotes are appearing. They have also been spotted in many citys around North America. One even recently found itsself on the roof of a bar in Queens, New York!

DAY 2

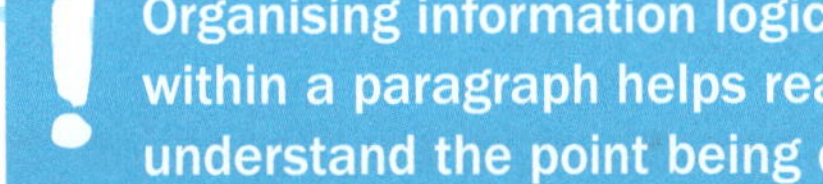

! Organising information logically within a paragraph helps readers understand the point being discussed.

Fill in the gaps to complete the paragraph outlines below.

a Topic sentence: Sloths are the world's slowest animals.

Supporting point 1: why sloths are so slow

Supporting point 2: the advantages of being slow

Supporting point 3: ______________________________

b Topic sentence: Animals can become extinct because of natural or human-made causes.

Supporting point 1: ______________________________

Supporting point 2: ______________________________

Supporting point 3: which is more common – natural or human-made causes?

DAY 3

Edit the informative piece below by correcting the four ending punctuation errors.

WICKED WEB-SLINGERS

Forget plastic, steel or concrete – it turns out that the humble spider creates the most versatile material on Earth – The spider's web is strong, flexible and sticky, with a range of applications, In fact, doing 'whatever a spider can' means a whole lot more than catching flies in cobwebs. *Hyptiotes cavatus*, or the triangle weaver spider, uses its special stretchy silk as a slingshot to propel itself towards its prey. The diving bell spider, *Argyroneta aquatica*, constructs special web vessels in which it can spend long periods of time underwater Scientists have even observed spiders using their webs to create silken balloons that allow them to 'fly'?

DAY 4

Reorder the supporting sentences into the most logical order to complete the paragraph. Add transition words (such as 'also', 'however' or 'as well') where appropriate.

- Bees pollinate plants that are fed to cattle, meaning they are important for the meat and dairy industries.
- Bees help to produce resources, such as beeswax, that are used in other products.
- The greatest contribution bees make is pollinating plants that produce fruits and vegetables.

WHY BEES ARE IMPORTANT

Bees perform many important functions. ______________________________

____

____

____

____

____

DAY 5

1 Edit the informative piece below by correcting the four spelling errors and the four ending punctuation errors.

KOALA PRINTS

Detectives looking into crimes in Australia will now need to eliminate a new suspect during the coarse of their investigations: the koala? According to recent research, Australia's beloved marsupial has fingerprints that are almost identical to that off humans Scientists say that the spirals and ridges on both the koala and the human fingerprint are almost inpossible to distinguish, even under a microscope? Although koalas aren't the only animals with fingerprints, they are one of the more mischievous creatures out there. Ask any Australian and they'll tell you to reguard koalas with caution and suspicion at all times –

2 Select an animal of your choice and complete a report on it.

Animal: ____________________

a This animal is found in ____________________.

b The physical appearance of this animal is best described as ____________________

____________________.

c This animal's diet consists of ____________________

____________________.

d This animal's relationship with humans is ____________________

____________________.

e Another interesting fact about this animal is that ____________________

____

____________________.

DAY 1

Edit the informative piece below by correcting the six capitalisation errors.

THE GIANT WATER LILY

From Anacondas to Jaguars, things are big in the Amazon rainforest, and the giant water lily is no exception. a flowering plant found in the shallow waters of the Amazon basin, the *Victoria amazonica* can produce up to ten flowers at a time. Each flower can grow to almost three metres wide. In addition to its incredible size, the giant lily is also very strong. Its flat leaves are supported by a long stalk that can hold the weight of an average-sized person. The plant's size caused a sensation when it was brought to europe in the Nineteenth century, where it is still grown in specially designed Hothouses today.

DAY 2

Each sentence in a paragraph should advance the argument and expand upon the previous point.

Write a sentence that advances the argument and expands on the point of the sentences below. The first one has been done for you.

a A large number of plants are in danger of becoming extinct.

Because plants can't flee when their habitats are being destroyed, they are more vulnerable than animals.

b Many medicines come from plant extracts.

____

____

c Plants absorb sunlight to produce energy and release oxygen into the air.

____

____

DAY 3

Edit the informative piece below by correcting the six comma errors (four in the wrong place, two missing).

THE CORPSE FLOWER

Despite its name the corpse flower (*Amorphophallus titanum*) isn't deadly – it just smells dead. This large flowering plant from Sumatra in Indonesia, takes its unusual title from the unpleasant odour it releases, during bloom. The stench is often compared to the smell of rotting meat (or, more precisely, a rotting dead body). It is designed to attract insects such as dung beetles flesh-eating flies and other carnivorous bugs so that they will pollinate the plant. But those brave enough to approach this beautiful plant, will need to be quick. The corpse flower blooms rarely and only under specific conditions. On average, a mature plant will come into flower for just two to three days, every thirty to forty years before shedding its leaves and collapsing.

DAY 4

Fill in the gaps with a sentence that supports the point of the previous sentence. The first one has been done for you.

Flowers are important because they have a positive psychological effect on people. The most pleasant aspect of a flower is its mix of colours and greenery. *Seeing these colours at home or in the office can help reduce stress*. Studies have confirmed that having flowers around makes people happier. This is especially true when they are given as a gift.

____

____.

The simple act of caring for flowers can also make people feel positive. ____________________

____

____.

DAY 5

❶ **Edit the informative piece below by correcting the five capitalisation errors and five comma errors (two in the wrong place, three missing).**

THE STRANGLER FIG

The strangler fig is the kind of guest that always overstays its welcome. native to tropical rainforests, in asia australasia and the americas this species of plant is dropped onto unsuspecting trees as a sticky seed. It then grows long roots around its host to 'strangle' it to death and take its place. Despite this gruesome fact strangler figs play an important role in the rainforest ecosystem. the spaces between the strangler figs' root systems provide shelter, for many animals, including bats and birds.

❷ **Using some or all of the points below as a guide, write a paragraph explaining the importance of trees. Remember to begin with an original topic sentence and to make each supporting point advance the point of the previous sentence.**

- Trees produce oxygen.
- Trees trap carbon dioxide, helping to counteract carbon emissions.
- Trees provide protection from direct sunlight.
- Parks with trees are nice places to walk and exercise.

DAY 1

Edit the informative piece below by correcting the eight spelling errors.

THE LOCH NESS MONSTER

The Loch Ness monster (or Nessie) is a mithical creature believed to inhibit Loch Ness, a large lake near Inverness, Scotland. References to an enormus beast living in the lake are found in early Scottish history, with many sightings of the creature being reported since that time. Accordding to those who clame to have seen it, Nessie is said to resembal a dinosaur with a long neck. One theory is that the creature could be the last survivor of a marine reptile species that is thought to have become extinc around 65.5 million years ago. However, there is no definitive prufe that the Loch Ness monster exists. In the end, it remains a mystery to us all.

DAY 2

Fill in the gaps with the most appropriate transition word or phrase for a concluding sentence, choosing from the options below.

! Concluding statements draw together the information presented in the rest of the paragraph, and are usually signposted using transition words or phrases.

thus | overall | given these points | interestingly | finally | for the most part | as can be seen | to summarise | on the whole | consequently

a ____________________________, the Egyptian myth of the sun god Ra can be interpreted as a reflection on how people use power.

b The Japanese myth of Izanagi and Izanami, ____________________________, would have been used to explain the beginning of the universe.

c ____________________________, the Roman myth of Cupid poses thoughtful questions about love and attraction.

d ____________________________, stories of the Greek hero Odysseus often fail to take into account the role of his wife, Penelope.

DAY 3

Edit the informative piece below by correcting the four apostrophe errors (three in the wrong place, one missing).

THE BUNYIP

The bunyip is a mythical water-dwelling creature from Aboriginal Australian folklore. While the creature's name and characteristic's differ according to different communities, it has been variously described as both ox-like and human in appearance, with webbed feet and claws. It is said to inhabit rivers and billabongs, and is rumoured to prey on unsuspecting women and children when they get too close to the waters edge. The Europeans' who arrived in Australia were unsure whether the bunyip was real or a myth, and they eventually came to fear the creature. This ultimately led to the bunyip cementing it's place in Australian mythology.

DAY 4

Write a concluding statement for each short paragraph below.

a One purpose of myths is to explain facts. These facts can be about the natural world or about human history. They are often explained in story form, rather than as a simple statement. ______________________________

____

______________________________.

b Although myths often refer to old stories and people from the past, today's leaders also create myths about themselves. They exaggerate their achievements in order to impress people. ______________________________

____

______________________________.

DAY 5

❶ **Edit the informative piece below by correcting the three spelling errors and the three apostrophe errors (two in the wrong place, one missing).**

THE LEGEND OF NIAN

There's a mythical monster from Chinese mythology called Nian that you may not have herd about. According to the original legend, the creature – described as half lion, half bull – lived in the mountains of China. Every year, it would desend to terrorise and hunt people in the villages below. One day, after banding together, the villager's confronted the monster. They dressed in red, beating their drums loudly and setting off fireworks to scare it away. Thats widely thought to be the origen of the Chinese New Year celebrations' as they are practised around the world today.

❷ **Fill in the gaps for a myth of your choice.**

a Myth: ______________________________ (e.g. Medusa, Thor)

b What is the story? ______________________________

____

____

c Why is it memorable? ______________________________

____

____

❸ **Write a concluding statement for the report you have completed above.**

In summary, ______________________________

____

______________________________.

DAY 1

Edit the informative piece below by correcting the four ending punctuation errors.

MAMI WATA

The water spirit Mami Wata is celebrated in many parts of Africa Her name means 'water mother', although in most traditions she has no children of her own, In paintings and sculptures she often has the head and upper body of a woman, and the tail of a fish – like a mermaid – She is a very complicated spirit, with both good and bad qualities. Sometimes she captures people who are swimming or in a boat and drags them away underwater. If they are lucky, she might let them return safely to dry land; after this they receive good fortune, becoming wealthier and happier? However, her scary qualities are never far away: Mami Wata can be blamed for all kinds of illness and bad luck.

DAY 2

Fill in the gap with a concluding statement that links to the topic sentence of the following paragraph.

A concluding statement can link to the topic sentence of the next paragraph.

Body paragraph 1: In some African mythologies evil spirits are believed to cause misfortune and illness to people. They are thought to play cruel tricks that cause harm and can even possess the bodies of people to do their bidding. There are many people who believe that these spirits actually exist. ______________________________

____

______________________________.

Topic sentence for body paragraph 2: There are spiritual professionals who communicate with spirits to protect against evil spirits.

Daily WRITING & EDITING Practice

DAY 3

Edit the informative piece below by correcting the seven spelling errors.

THE FATES

The Fates are three goddesses who weave the destinies of all beings. They our part of many mythological traditions: the best known are the Moirai of ainchent Greek mythology. Together they create a tapestry that controls the lives of humans and of the many Greek gods. The three goddesses have different roles: one spins the thread of life, another meazures the amount of thread for each person and the third cuts the thread, determineing when and how that person will dye. Although most people like to think they have control over there lives, we can still see the influence of the Fates in frases such as 'the tapestry of life' and 'weaving your destiny'.

DAY 4

Highlight the most effective concluding statement in each pair and explain your choice.

a To sum up, the Roman god Jupiter had an interesting run-in with a bee.

In the end, the story of Jupiter and the bee reveals the negative consequences of revenge.

Explanation: ____

____.

b On the whole, Durga's defeat of Mahisha, the fierce buffalo demon, represents the idea of destruction.

In the end, Durga cuts off the buffalo demon's head.

Explanation: ____

____.

DAY 5

❶ **Edit the informative piece below by correcting the three ending punctuation errors and the three spelling errors.**

ROBIN HOOD

The stories about Robin Hood, the legendery figure who stole from the rich and gave to the poor, are hundreds of years old? He lived in the 1200s, in Sherwood Forest in Nottinghamshire, England Robin Hood was an outlaw, meaning he committed crimes and had to avoid being captured – which is why he lived in the forest. Helping him were his band of Merry Men, especially Little John (who was actualy very tall). However, he was on the side of the common people and was the enemy of the Sheriff, who forced them to pay high taxes. So, although Robin Hood was a criminal, he is regarded as brave, heroick and a champion of the people/

❷ **Write a paragraph on a mythical figure or creature of your choice. Do not use the same figure you wrote about in Week 17, Day 5. Remember, the concluding statement should sum up the main points of the paragraph.**

DAY 1

Edit the persuasive piece below by correcting the six comma errors (two in the wrong place, four missing).

WHAT'S THE BEST SCHOOL SUBJECT?

In my opinion, the best school subject is Physical Education (PE) because it is not confined to the classroom and it is good for your health. Unlike most other subjects, where you have to sit and listen to the teacher for the whole class PE allows you to go outside breathe in some fresh air and stretch your muscles. Furthermore, PE teaches the importance of physical health – an important life lesson that all children should learn. Studies have shown, that performing physical activities helps people to concentrate better and maintain focus for longer. So the exercises done in PE classes from push-ups to playing basketball actually help students perform better, in academic subjects.

DAY 2

Fill in the gaps explaining why your favourite school subject is the best. (If PE is your favourite school subject, write on your second-favourite subject.)

! A complete paragraph consists of a topic sentence, supporting points and a concluding statement.

Topic sentence: ______________________________

______________________________.

Supporting point 1: ______________________________

______________________________.

Supporting point 2: ______________________________

______________________________.

Concluding statement: ______________________________

______________________________.

DAY 3

Edit the persuasive piece below by correcting the six verb errors. The first three have been done for you.

WHAT'S THE BEST SPORT?

I ~~will~~ believe that the best sport is target archery because it ~~improved~~ *improves* hand–eye coordination and helps increase focus. Archery ~~required~~ *requires* you to perform two functions at once: holding a bow and arrow using the correct technique and using your sight to aimed at the target. Repeatedly shooting arrows at the target trains your hands and eyes to work together. Practising this skill also helped improve concentration, as target archery requires your full attention in order to succeed. You needed to tune out your surroundings in order to focus on standing in the correct position and hitting the target. Although target archery is not the most physically gruelling sport, it requires both strength and precision.

DAY 4

Fill in the gaps explaining why your favourite sport (or hobby) is the best. (If target archery is your favourite sport, write on your second-favourite sport.)

Topic sentence: ______________________________

______________________________.

Supporting point 1: ______________________________

______________________________.

Supporting point 2: ______________________________

______________________________.

Concluding statement: ______________________________

______________________________.

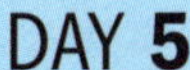

DAY 5

❶ **Edit the persuasive piece below by correcting the four comma errors (two in the wrong place, two missing) and the four verb errors.**

WHAT'S THE BEST GENRE OF MUSIC?

The lasting influence and funky dance feel of disco music, make this genre of music the best. Although disco music was not as popular as it once was its influence can still be heard in popular music today. Used by artists such as Lady Gaga and heard in songs like Dua Lipa's 'Don't Start Now', the trademark sounds of disco music (for example reverberated vocals) was alive and well. And disco music is so much fun to dance to! Before disco exploding onto the New York City scene in the late 1960s, social dancing was only performs by couples. Disco dancing was the first time people could go on the dance floor, as individuals and dance in crowds. Disco was a game-changer, and for this reason it is the best genre of music.

❷ **Write a complete paragraph explaining why your favourite genre of music is the best. (If disco is your favourite genre of music, write on your second-favourite genre.)**

DAY 1

Edit the persuasive piece below by correcting the seven apostrophe errors (two in the wrong place, five missing).

WHY DOGS ARE BETTER THAN CATS

Its simply a fact, one that cannot be argued against by any logical person: dog's are fun to play with, they promote an active lifestyle and, for these reasons, they are undeniably superior to cats. Cats can sometimes be fun. Theyll play with string and bat their cat toys around. But dogs absolutely love to play. There's fetch, chase, tug-of-war and even doggie play dates! Cats just don't have the same mindset. Theyre solitary creatures who like their alone time. Theyd much rather stay at home and do their own thing, whereas dogs love to be outside running with their humans. Dogs put smiles on peoples faces' and are an integral part of the family unit.

DAY 2

Each paragraph should thoroughly explore one distinct idea.

Provide the main idea for three paragraphs in response to the topic below. The first one has been done for you.

STUDENTS SHOULD NOT BE ALLOWED TO CHOOSE THEIR TEACHERS

Main idea 1: *Allowing students to choose their teacher is not preparing them well for the future. In the real world, people are not allowed to choose their boss or their colleagues. People need to learn how to get along with others, and this starts at school.*

Main idea 2: ____________________

____

____________________.

Main idea 3: ____________________

____

____________________.

DAY 3

Edit the persuasive piece below by correcting the five comma errors (two in the wrong place, three missing).

WHY PINEAPPLE DOES NOT BELONG ON PIZZA

No self-respecting pizza lover – or at least one who values tradition good cuisine and being on the right side of history – could possibly enjoy pineapple on pizza. Pizza is defined in the Oxford English Dictionary, as 'a dish of Italian origin consisting of a flat round base of dough baked with a topping of tomatoes and cheese, typically with added meat fish or vegetables'. Pineapple is not a meat fish or vegetable and therefore should not technically be used as a pizza topping. But leaving accuracy and logic aside, the mere taste of sweet pineapple chunks (and their juice!) mixed with savoury ingredients, should be enough to ward against this foul concoction.

DAY 4

Fill in the gap to complete the topic below and provide the main idea for three paragraphs in response to the topic.

____________________ **IS THE BEST SUPERPOWER**

Main idea 1: ______________________________

____

____.

Main idea 2: ______________________________

____

____.

Main idea 3: ______________________________

____

____.

DAY 5

❶ **Edit the persuasive piece below by correcting the three apostrophe errors (two in the wrong place, one missing) and the three comma errors (one in the wrong place, two missing).**

WHY HANDWRITING IS STILL IMPORTANT

Many people think that handwriting is outdated in todays digital age, but these people fail to take into account the many benefits of writing by hand. First, handwriting reinforces reading and language-processing skills. When we write by hand, we have more time to think about the words that are being written how they are spelt and how we are constructing meaning for readers. Second, using pen and paper allows more freedom when doing things such as brainstorming. There are no restrictions: you have the whole page to make links' between points add side note's and be as creative as you like. There'll always be a place for handwriting, in our modern world.

❷ **Fill in the gap to complete the topic below and write one complete paragraph in response to the topic.**

YOUNGER SIBLINGS ____________________ BE FORCED TO LISTEN TO THEIR OLDER SIBLINGS

____

____

____

____

____

____

____

____

____

STRUCTURING RESPONSES

Daily checklist

WEEK	DAY 1	DAY 2	DAY 3	DAY 4	DAY 5
21	☐	☐	☐	☐	☐
22	☐	☐	☐	☐	☐
23	☐	☐	☐	☐	☐
24	☐	☐	☐	☐	☐
25	☐	☐	☐	☐	☐
26	☐	☐	☐	☐	☐
27	☐	☐	☐	☐	☐
28	☐	☐	☐	☐	☐
29	☐	☐	☐	☐	☐
30	☐	☐	☐	☐	☐

DAY 1

Edit the block-structured piece below by correcting the six spelling errors.

POKÉMON VS DIGIMON

One of the most popular anime shows of the 1990s was *Pokémon*. Initialley designed as a video game, *Pokémon* has expanded into many other areas, including television, film and tradeing cards. Pokémon (or Pocket Monsters) refers to the cartoon monsters that are caught and used in battel by Pokémon trainers. In the television series, the main character, Ash Ketchum, travells the world with his best friend, Pikachu, trying to 'catch 'em all'.

Another popular anime show during the 1990s was *Digimon*. It is similer to *Pokémon* in that it also began as a video game and features stories about children and strange creatures. Unlike *Pokémon*, which follows the journey of Ash without end, *Digimon* had a story ark that would finish after each season, usually with the defeat of the main villain.

DAY 2

Complete the block-approach response below. (The block approach is good for talking about separate topics, one by one.)

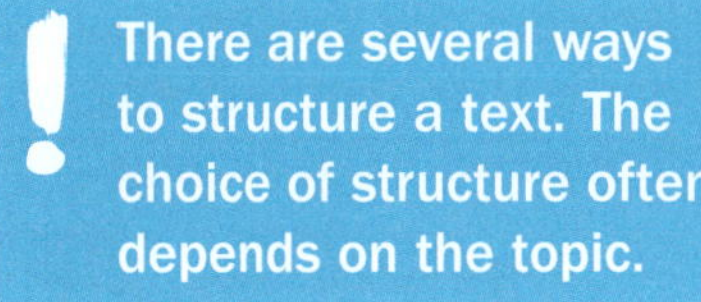

Facebook is a social networking platform where users can create profiles, post comments, share photographs and post links to news or other interesting content. There are also functions to chat with friends and watch short-form videos. Although the primary purpose of the platform is to help friends reconnect, it is also used as a means for businesses to send targeted ads to people.

Another social networking platform is ________________ (e.g. Instagram, TikTok).

____

____

____

____

DAY 3

Edit the chronologically structured piece below by correcting the five verb errors.

A SHORT HISTORY OF THE PARALYMPICS

Before the Paralympics existed, sporting clubs in Berlin will hold competitions for hearing-impaired athletes as far back as 1888. Following the end of World War II in 1945, Dr Ludwig Guttmann notice a large number of injured soldiers and civilians, and he will propose the idea of holding wheelchair competitions to make their rehabilitation more enjoyable. The first is held during the London Olympics in England in 1948 and was named the Stoke Mandeville Games. Sixteen war veterans competed for victory. The Netherlands also take part in the games in 1952, and by 1960 in Rome 400 athletes from 23 countries competed. The games in Rome were considered the first official Paralympic Games in history.

DAY 4

Reorder the sentences below to form a chronologically structured paragraph, moving from earliest to most recent information. Add transition words and phrases (such as 'next', 'however' or 'following') where appropriate.

- There are several stories that are often recognised as the first Western fairytales.
- More than a hundred years later, Hans Christian Andersen published the popular *Fairy Tales for Children*.
- The exact date of the first recorded fairytale is unknown.
- In 1697, Charles Perrault published *Cinderella* and *The Sleeping Beauty*.

Fairytales are traditional stories that have been passed down for centuries. ______________________

____

____

____

____

____

____

DAY 5

❶ **Edit the sequentially structured piece below by correcting the three spelling errors and the three verb errors.**

SO YOU WANT TO MAKE A PODCAST?

In order to make a chart-topping podcast, you have to start with a catchy name. Thought of something funny, misterious or clever to make potential listeners want to listen to your podcast immediately. Next, choose attractive cover artwork, and writing an enticing description that tells listeners why they should tune in. Depending on your style, you can write talking points or a script to follow so that your show stays focused. Now that you're ready to record, found a quiet place without noise or interupptions! Next, edit your recording and upload it to a hosting service. Finally, promote your podcast through popular streaming platforms such as Spotify, so that everyone can here what you have to say.

❷ **Select which structure (block, chronological, sequential/step-by-step) is most appropriate for each topic and explain your choice.**

a A biography of civil rights activist Rosa Parks

Structure: ______________________________

Explanation: ______________________________

____

b Instructions on how to build a website

Structure: ______________________________

Explanation: ______________________________

____

c Similarities and differences between primary school and secondary school

Structure: ______________________________

Explanation: ______________________________

____

DAY 1

Edit the block-structured piece below by correcting the five ending punctuation errors.

AUSTRALIA'S POLITICAL PARTIES

The Australian Labor Party (also known as the ALP) is one of the two main political parties in Australia? It is the oldest Australian political party and operates on federal, state and local government levels Its main concerns include healthcare, the environment and education. The ALP is known for having the country's first and only female Prime Minister: Julia Gillard.

The Liberal Party of Australia was founded in 1944 and is the other main political party in Australia. The Liberal Party also operates at all three levels of government, Its main concerns include the economy, defence, and law and order The Liberal Party is known for having the country's longest-serving Prime Minister: Robert Menzies –

DAY 2

Fill in the gaps to a pair of topics, then describe one similarity and one difference between the two things.

! Regardless of how a piece of writing is structured, it must address the topic.

a Australia and ______________________

Similarity: ______________________

____

Difference: ______________________

____

b ______________________ and birthdays

Similarity: ______________________

____

Difference: ______________________

____

DAY 3

Edit the chronologically structured piece below by correcting the six verb errors.

A SHORT HISTORY OF EMOJIS

Emojis will start off as emoticons (emotion icons), simple faces created using punctuation marks such as brackets and colons. Their first known use was in 1881 in *Puck* magazine, which introduce emoticons for the feelings of joy, sadness and surprise. In 1982, emoticons become popular on an online bulletin board, where a smiling or frowning emoticon was used to indicating whether a post was serious or a joke. Emoticons became emojis ('picture characters' in Japanese) in the 1990s after Shigetaka Kurita, an engineer at a Japanese phone company, developed 176 characters to be used in text messages. Since then, the popularity of emojis will continue to rise, and in 2015 the Oxford English Dictionary name the 'face with tears of joy' emoji as the word of the year.

DAY 4

Imagine a timeline for your future.

By the end of this year: ______________________________

____

Next year: ______________________________

____

In five years: ______________________________

____

____

In ten years: ______________________________

____

____

DAY 5

❶ **Edit the sequentially structured piece below by correcting the three ending punctuation errors and the three verb errors.**

RECYCLING

Recycling is an important part of taking care of the environment It referred to the process of collecting and processing materials that would otherwise be thrown away as trash, and turning them into new products. There were three steps involved in recycling, and these steps form a loop. Step one is to collect1 Methods of collection vary from community to community, but usually include kerbside collection and drop-off centres. Step two is manufacturing? The cleaned and sorted recyclables are processed and used to produce items such as paper towels and plastic containers. Step three is purchasing. The recycling loop continues by people purchase new products made from recycled materials, which can then be recycled again.

❷ **Write a complete paragraph on one of the topics below using one of the structures listed.**

Topic: history of my school | PlayStation vs Xbox | how to ride a bicycle

Structure: block | sequential | chronological

DAY 1

Edit this introduction to a persuasive piece by correcting the six capitalisation errors.

STREAMING SERVICES VERSUS FREE-TO-AIR TV

Television streaming services have become very popular in many households. No longer does the family sit in the Lounge Room each evening watching the nightly news, followed by a drama series. These days, people like to watch what they want, when they want. Free-to-air Channels simply cannot compete with the number and variety of programs provided by streaming services. Additionally, companies like netflix and amazon create their own high-quality drama series. best of all, streaming services don't interrupt your favourite programs and movies with ads every five minutes. In any comparison of the two, streaming is clearly far superior.

DAY 2

! An introduction to a persuasive text must provide a contention (i.e. an opinion) in response to the topic. It must also give reasons for this opinion.

1. **Highlight a statement in the introduction above that clearly expresses an opinion on whether streaming or free-to-air TV is better.**

2. **Summarise the three main reasons why the writer prefers streaming services.**

   Supporting reason 1: Streaming TV provides ______________________

   than free-to-air TV.

   Supporting reason 2: The quality of programs is better on ______________________

   than on ______________________.

   Supporting reason 3: ______________________

   ______________________.

3. **Write down your opinion on whether streaming or free-to-air TV is better, and why.**

   ____

   ____

Daily WRITING & EDITING Practice

DAY 3

Edit this introduction to a persuasive piece by correcting the six comma errors (three in the wrong place, three missing).

SUMMER VERSUS WINTER

There are four seasons in the year but spring and autumn are fairly similar. They have moderate temperatures and the lengths of days and nights are about the same. It is summer and winter, that divide opinions. Some people like the blazing heat the ice-cool drinks and the long hours of sunlight, that summer brings. Others though prefer winter, snuggling up indoors in front of the heater with something warm, to eat and drink. Both summer and winter offer much to enjoy – it is the balance of these two seasons that makes the journey through the year so rich and varied.

DAY 4

Provide a contention (i.e. an opinion) for each of the topics below. The first one has been done for you.

a Comedy versus drama: *These two genres are completely different but their individual strengths make each of them enjoyable to watch, depending on your mood.*

b Land versus sea: ____________________

c City versus country: ____________________

d Childhood versus adulthood: ____________________

e Human versus machine: ____________________

DAY 5

1 Edit the persuasive piece below by correcting the three capitalisation errors and the three comma errors (one in the wrong place, two missing).

THE RISKS OF SOCIAL MEDIA USE

in our increasingly connected digital world, social media platforms such as Facebook, Twitter and Instagram pose enormous risks, to users of all ages. One of these risks is cyberbullying a form of harassment using Electronic means. Another risk of using social media is the effect of negative thoughts that users can have when they compare themselves to the supposedly Perfect online personas of social media influencers. While there are many positive aspects of social media, such as keeping friends and family connected and providing useful information these risks need to be taken seriously.

2 Provide three reasons that support a contention you wrote for one of the topics from Day 4.

Supporting reason 1: ________________________________

Supporting reason 2: ________________________________

Supporting reason 3: ________________________________

3 Using your answers from Question 2, write a short introduction in response to the topic. Remember to state your opinion (i.e. your contention) clearly.

DAY 1

Edit the imaginative piece below by correcting the six quotation mark errors (two in the wrong place, four missing).

THE TEST

Tristan and Flora crept to the edge of the farm and shuffled quietly into the abandoned shed. The whistling wind continued to blow outside. Flora nestled her nose deeper into her scarf to stop herself from shivering.

'Hurry up, Tristan.' It's freezing. Just tell me what you have to tell me and let's get out of here. 'Old McDougall's farm at night gives me the heebie-jeebies.'

Tristan held out his hands and clumsily removed his thick gloves. You're not going to believe this. I'm not sure I believe it myself yet ... Just promise you won't scream.

Flora nodded, sure that there was nothing her best friend could show her that would scare her. Suddenly Tristan's hands erupted into scorching orange flames.

'OMG! Flora looked at her friend in shock. What ... are you?'

DAY 2

Develop an idea for your own story by completing the table below.

The orientation (or beginning) sets the scene, introduces the main characters and suggests what the story is going to be about.

	THE TEST	YOUR STORY
When?	At night	
Where?	Old McDougall's farm	
Who?	Tristan and Flora (best friends)	
What?	Tristan reveals to Flora that he has developed powers that allow him to produce flames from his hands.	

DAY 3

Edit the imaginative piece below by correcting the five apostrophe errors (one in the wrong place, four missing).

TO THE CIRCUS WE GO: SCENE I

Deni, 15, and her older sister Olga, 17, sneak out of the house.

Deni: Are you sure about this, Olga? What if Mum and Dad catch us? Well be grounded forever.

Olga: Stop being such a baby, Deni! Youre the one who wanted to do this, remember. You kept saying it was your dream to become an acrobat in the circus'. Well, if you don't go for this audition, youll be stuck in this town for the rest of your life. Stuck doing something boring that you hate and wasting all your talent.

Deni: Wow ... I had no idea you believed in me so much ... Okay, then. Lets do it!

DAY 4

Complete the description below for the story idea you developed in Day 2.

This story is set in ______________________ (place or time). It follows ______________________ (main character) as he/she tries to ______________________

____

______________________ (character goal). The main character can be described as ______________________ and ______________________

______________________ . The most interesting aspect of the main character is ______________________

______________________ .

The orientation of the story will draw readers in because ______________________

____

______________________ .

Daily **WRITING & EDITING** Practice

DAY 5

❶ **Edit the imaginative piece below by correcting the three quotation mark errors (three missing) and the three apostrophe errors (one in the wrong place, two missing).**

TREASURE ADVENTURE

The dinghy smashes into the sand with a thud. Mahesh and Bjorn fling themselves out of the boat and crumple to the ground.

'We are never doing that again,' Mahesh spits at Bjorn. Ever!

'It's not my fault it took so long,' Bjorn replies, breathing hard. 'Who knew that this stupid island is so big?'

The two friend's remain motionless on the sand for several minutes before Bjorn finally pushes himself up, shaking the sand out of his pants.

Well, were here now,' he says. 'I've got the map and our supplies, so what are we waiting for? Lets find some treasure!'

❷ **Using one of the prompts below or your story idea from Days 2 and 4, write an orientation (i.e. beginning) to an imaginative piece.**

- One friend tells another they are moving to a different country
- Time travel to a future world
- A mystery

DAY 1

Edit this body paragraph for a persuasive piece by correcting the five verb errors.

The introduction to this text is on page 73.

STREAMING SERVICES VERSUS FREE-TO-AIR TV

There was an astonishingly large number and variety of programs you can watch on any streaming service. These will include sitcoms, drama series and lifestyle shows, as well as movies and documentaries. Although this isn't too different from traditional TV, streaming services provided much more choice. In 2018, Business Insider Australia reported that there were 5579 movies and TV shows available on Netflix. Also, a lot of international sport is now only available on streaming services such as Foxtel Now, while just a few of the new TV series and movies created by the streaming companies were on free-to-air networks. For the amount and variety of content, streaming was the best way to watch TV.

DAY 2

Fill in the gaps with the most appropriate word or phrase from the word bank below to introduce examples and evidence. Finish the paragraph with a strong concluding statement.

! Body paragraphs expand on the reasons listed in the introduction, adding examples and evidence.

for example	also	including	as well as	such as	furthermore

One reason why reading a book is much better than watching the movie adaptation is that the book includes much more detail and information. ________________, minor characters are often left out of the movie version. ________________, background information, ________________ details of the characters' pasts, is usually summed up quickly in a film, whereas a book might devote whole chapters to describing the characters' history. A film might ________________ leave out key dialogue that would help us to understand characters. These examples all show that ____

____.

DAY 3

Edit this body paragraph for a persuasive piece by correcting the seven capitalisation errors.
The introduction to this text is on page 74.

SUMMER VERSUS WINTER

Summer offers many opportunities to enjoy the Great Outdoors. The school holidays, the generally fine weather and the long Daylight hours all combine to create chances to relax and have family time in the fresh air. whether it is a morning at the beach, a game of backyard cricket or an evening Barbecue, there are many ways to be healthy and active. Yet summer also brings bushfires and dangerous heat, flies and mosquitoes, and harsh sun. Furthermore, this season can be very hectic. the summer Months are usually full of rushing around, last-minute preparations for visitors or holiday travel and squeezing in catch-ups with friends and relatives.

DAY 4

Provide two examples or pieces of evidence to build an outline of two body paragraphs. The first one has been done for you.

COMEDY VERSUS DRAMA

Topic sentence: Comedy programs and films make people happy.

First example / piece of evidence: *Comedies are lighthearted and entertaining, so they can help audiences forget about their worries.*

Second example / piece of evidence: ______________________________

____

Topic sentence: Drama series and films make people think.

First example / piece of evidence: ______________________________

____

Second example / piece of evidence: ______________________________

____

Daily WRITING & EDITING Practice

DAY 5

❶ **Edit this body paragraph for a persuasive piece by correcting the three verb errors and the three capitalisation errors.** The introduction to this text is on page 75.

THE RISKS OF SOCIAL MEDIA USE

Users need to be aware of the negative aspects of social media. Cyberbullying was a big issue, involving online threats and aggressive or rude posts or messages. bullies may use fake profiles to remain anonymous and victims, who can now be contacted via social media at any time of day, can feel as if there is no escape. Furthermore, social media platforms such as instagram allowing users to share the best aspects of themselves and hide anything negative, creating a facade of perfection. This sets an unrealistic standard for their followers to try to live up to, making them feel inadequate in comparison. while these risks are enough to scare anyone away from using social media, there were ways to minimise the dangers and enjoy all that the internet has to offer.

❷ **Write a complete body paragraph that expands on one of the supporting reasons you provided in Week 23, Day 5, Question 2. Remember to introduce examples and evidence using the appropriate words.**

DAY 1

Edit the imaginative piece below by correcting the five quotation mark errors (two in the wrong place, three missing). The beginning of this story is on page 76.

THE TEST

The flames that had moments ago covered Tristan's hands began to dwindle like the last embers in a fireplace. Flora might've convinced herself that it was all just a mirage if it hadn't been for the last wisps of smoke spiralling from her best friend's fingers.

'What happened to you? she stuttered. Tristan looked at Flora, the one person he had dared to share this terrible secret with. He saw nothing but fear in her eyes.

I have no idea,' he said, fumbling with his gloves as he hurriedly tried to cover his unharmed hands. That's why I had to tell you. 'I'm so scared. I need your help.'

'Flora looked away, tears beginning to stream down her face like droplets of rain on a car window. 'I don't know if I can be friends with … a freak. I'm sorry.'

DAY 2

> **!** A complication is an unexpected challenge or obstacle. It disrupts the story and causes further interesting events.

1. **In your own words, describe the complication in the story above.**

   ____

   ____

2. **How does the complication progress the story or add interest for readers?**

   ____

   ____

3. **A simile compares two things using 'like' or 'as' to create a word picture. Highlight the two similes in the story above.**

4. **Complete the similes below using a phrase of your choice.**

   a The flames erupted like ______________________________ .

   b Flora ran as fast as ______________________________ .

Daily WRITING & EDITING Practice

DAY 3

Edit the imaginative piece below by correcting the five ending punctuation errors.
The beginning of this story is on page 77.

TO THE CIRCUS WE GO: SCENE II

Deni and Olga arrive at the circus, where they are greeted by a clown in a pink-and-green suit.

Deni: [*Excitedly*] Hello; My name is Deni Velour. I'm here to audition to be an acrobat.

Clown: I'm sorry, my dear. Auditions closed twenty minutes ago. [*Honks his nose twice.*] I have a better idea? Be a clown, be a clown All the world loves a clown!

Olga: What? No! My sister has been dreaming about being a world-famous acrobat her whole life; she's the best there is. Why in the world would she want to be a clown and wear some silly pink-and-green suit.

Deni: Please I know the circus doesn't accept new acrobats very often. This might be my only chance to get out of this town ...

DAY 4

Imagine a complication for each of the story ideas below.

Orientation	Complication
Jill, a pianist, auditions for a prestigious music school.	
Cleo asks Sam out on a date.	
Ramon and his family go to the jungle.	
Mary discovers a time-travel machine.	

DAY 5

1 Edit the imaginative piece below by correcting the three quotation mark errors (two in the wrong place, one missing) and the three ending punctuation errors. The beginning of this story is on page 78.

TREASURE ADVENTURE

Mahesh and Bjorn drag the dinghy up the beach and hide it among some ferns. Once they are happy that their only means of returning home is safely covered, the two friends set off into the heart of the island.

‘Are we going the right way.’ Mahesh asks Bjorn.

‘Of course we are, Bjorn huffs. ‘Don’t you think I know how to read a map.’

Mahesh shrugs, not entirely convinced, but continues to follow his friend. Bjorn leads them further and further away from the water until they eventually reach a crumbling castle.

‘We’re here?’ Bjorn exclaims.’

As he and Mahesh move towards the castle, a three-headed lion jumps out from the shadows. It roars loudly, sending Mahesh and Bjorn staggering back.’

2 Continue the story you started in Week 24, Day 5, Question 2 by introducing a complication. Try to include at least one simile in your story.

DAY 1

Edit this body paragraph for a persuasive piece by correcting the seven plural errors. The first three have been done for you. The previous paragraph of this text is on page 79.

STREAMING SERVICES VERSUS FREE-TO-AIR TV

One argument against streaming services ~~are~~ *is* the cost. When you pay for a ~~subscriptions~~ *subscription*, if you want the biggest choice of ~~program~~ *programs* you need a more expensive plan and probably two or more service. In comparison, free-to-air TV is free for the viewer to watch. However, on a commercial TV station you are forced to watch the ads – around thirteen minute per hour, regularly interrupting your favourite show or movie. Some of these ads are for gambling, alcohol and other things that many parents do not want their children to be exposed to. Streaming service, though, are ad-free, and for many people the ad-free experience are worth paying for.

DAY 2

Fill in the gaps with an appropriate rebuttal statement. (Rebuttal is contradicting the argument or proving it wrong.) The first one has been done for you.

! Persuasive techniques (e.g. rebuttal, emotive language) are used to convince readers that the writer's opinion is correct.

a Some people argue that celebrities deserve more privacy. However, *celebrities enjoy earning money from being seen and heard in the media, so they do not deserve any more privacy*.

b Some people argue that the sport of boxing should be banned. In fact, ______________________________.

c Some people argue that professional sportspeople should not have to be role models. In reality, though, ______________________________.

d Some people argue that social media accounts should be available to children from the age of ten. However, ______________________________.

DAY 3

Edit this body paragraph from a persuasive piece by correcting the six comma errors (two in the wrong place, four missing). The previous paragraph of this text is on page 80.

SUMMER VERSUS WINTER

One of my favourite things to do on a grey winter afternoon is to visit a cafe – preferably with a roaring log fire – and settle into a comfy couch, with a hot chocolate a piece of cake and a magazine. Time seems to slow down and the luxurious warmth of the surroundings keeps the winter chills far away. Only in winter does there seem to be time for such restful contemplation. However, winter does have its downfalls, too. Going outside in freezing temperatures especially in the morning can be very uncomfortable. The sky is often grey and depressing, during winter and it gets darker much earlier leaving less time to enjoy the outdoors.

DAY 4

1. **In the passage above, highlight three words or phrases with positive associations that are used to describe winter. Circle three words or phrases with negative associations that are used to describe winter.**

2. **Fill in the gaps using an appropriate emotive word. (Emotive words carry a strong emotion and show how a writer is feeling about something.) The first one has been done for you.**

   One of the best things about winter is the food. Bowls of ___steamy___ porridge, hot ____________ soups and ____________ roast potatoes are regulars in our house. Summer offers a completely different selection. ____________ fresh fruit and ____________ garden salads are on offer day after day, which makes for a ____________, ____________ diet.

3. **Using emotive words, write a sentence describing your favourite season.**

   ____

   ____

DAY 5

❶ **Edit this body paragraph from a persuasive piece by correcting the three plural errors and the three comma errors (two in the wrong place, one missing).** **The previous paragraph of this text is on page 81.**

THE RISKS OF SOCIAL MEDIA USE

There is many ways to reduce or minimise the risks of negative impacts from social media use. While cyberbullying can be hard to avoid all social media platforms provide an option to report bullying behaviour and to block users, who act inappropriately. Users should only accept friend requests or messages, from people they know in real life. Also, young social media users can ask adult for help if they are experiencing cyberbullying. Additionally, users should always be aware that not everything they see on social media are accurate. Though people may display an idealised persona, in actuality they experience the realities of life such as fear and hardship like everyone else.

❷ **Write a complete body paragraph that expands on one of the supporting reasons you provided in Week 23, Day 5, Question 2. Do not repeat the same point you used in Week 25, Day 5, Question 2. Include rebuttal and use emotive language to persuade your audience to agree with your point of view.**

DAY 1

Edit the imaginative piece below by correcting the five comma errors (three in the wrong place, two missing). The previous part of this story is on page 82.

THE TEST

As Flora rushed out of the shed and into the biting cold air Tristan stood in shock. He could do nothing but watch, as his best friend ran away from him. The moment he needed her the most she had fled …

He knew this would be hard for anyone to take in. (It was hard for him, too!) But he had truly believed that Flora would understand what he was going through, or would at least try, to understand. Hadn't he been there when her parents had divorced? Or when Dipesh had dumped her the night before the big dance?

If she couldn't support him, when he really needed her, then maybe he didn't want to have her in his life, as hard as that was to admit.

DAY 2

Characterisation gives readers a strong sense of a character's personality. Good characterisation makes a story more interesting and compelling.

1. **What does the passage above reveal about Tristan and Flora?**

____

____

2. **Explain how each sentence below helps to develop Flora's character.**

a Flora stays up all night pacing her room, thinking about what happened.

____

____

b Flora turns on the TV and sees a burning house. She turns the TV off immediately.

____

____

DAY 3

Edit the imaginative piece below by correcting the five spelling errors. The previous part of this story is on page 83.

TO THE CIRCUS WE GO: SCENE III

Deni stands alone, staring at the circus tent. Olga continues to argue with the clown in the background.

Deni: It's so beutiful. It's everything I imagined it would be. Colourful, brite, full of joy. And it must be even more incredibal inside ... This is all my fault. If I hadn't needed Olga to convince me to come, we wouldn't have been late and I wouldn't have missed my one chance. I allways do this: shoot myself in the foot right when things are looking up.

Deni sees two young acrobats skiping out of the tent. They're smiling from ear to ear.

Deni: Why can't I be like them? They're so carefree and happy. That's all I've ever wanted to be. That, and an acrobat.

DAY 4

Complete the dialogue below between Olga and the clown to further develop their characters.

Olga: (*Angrily*) ______________________________

____

Clown: There's no need to get snippy with me, missy! Clowns have feelings too. ______________

____

Olga: I'm sorry, okay. This audition is just so important to both me and my sister. __________

____

Clown: I understand how you feel. ______________________________

____

DAY 5

❶ **Edit the imaginative piece below by correcting the three comma errors (three missing) and the three spelling errors.** **The previous part of this story is on page 84.**

TREASURE ADVENTURE

Mahesh and Bjorn watch as the creature tries to atack them but is pulled back by a chain around its neck.

'What is that?' Mahesh shrieks. 'Bjorn you didn't say anything about a three-headed lion guarding the treasure!'

'Oviously, I didn't know,' Bjorn replies, exasperatedly. 'What should we do? We can't turn back now can we? We're so close …'

'No, we're definitely not runing from this,' Mahesh says, standing tall. 'Between the two of us, we can outwit the lion sneak in and grab *our* treasure.'

'Yeah, you're right,' Bjorn says, standing shoulder to shoulder with his fellow adventurer. 'Let's show that thing what we're made of!'

❷ **Fill in the gaps for one of the main characters in your story from Week 26, Day 5, Question 2.**

Positive attributes: ____________________ (e.g. friendly, brave)

Negative attributes: ____________________ (e.g. angry, rude)

❸ **Continue your story from Week 26, Day 5, Question 2. Focus on one of the attributes you have listed above to further develop one of the main characters.**

____

____

____

____

____

____

____

DAY 1

Edit this conclusion to a persuasive piece by correcting the five plural errors. The previous paragraph of this text is on page 85.

STREAMING SERVICES VERSUS FREE-TO-AIR TV

Streaming services and free-to-air TV is similar in some ways, offering a mix of comedy and drama, movies and series, real-life and highly imaginative content. Yet in many ways their difference are more striking than their similarities. Streaming services offers variety, choice, quality and convenience. In contrast, free-to-air TV have a limited range of programs, and commercial stations have frequent and highly intrusive ad breaks. More and more, the most admired and popular programs is only available through a streaming service. Yes, there is a cost, but the benefits make the cost of streaming services well and truly worth it.

DAY 2

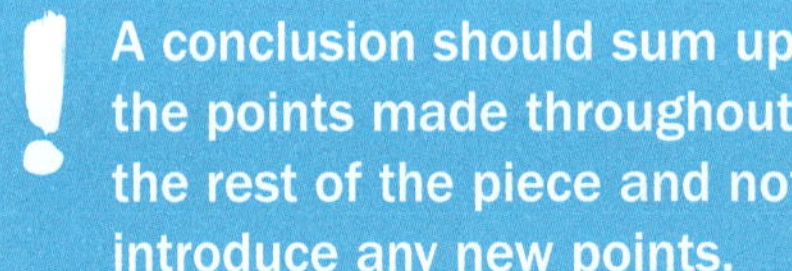

A conclusion should sum up the points made throughout the rest of the piece and not introduce any new points.

1. **Highlight the sentence in the conclusion above that best sums up the argument as a whole and underline two reasons that support this argument.**

2. **Write down two words or phrases from the conclusion that show the writer has a poor opinion of free-to-air TV.**

   ______________________, ______________________

3. **Write down two words or phrases from this conclusion that show the writer approves of streaming services.**

   ______________________, ______________________

4. **Do you think the conclusion above is a good or bad conclusion? Why?**

   ____

   ____

   ____

Daily WRITING & EDITING Practice

DAY 3

Edit this conclusion to a persuasive piece by correcting the six apostrophe errors (four in the wrong place, two missing). The previous paragraph of this text is on page 86.

SUMMER VERSUS WINTER

Overall, the many differences between summer and winter make it impossible for me to choose a clear favourite. Summer's have warm, sunny days, as well as extreme heat and savage bushfire's. Winter storm's can wreak havoc, yet a wild wind on a nature walk can clear away the mental cobwebs. A cool drink on a shady verandah is perfect on a summer's day, just as theres nothing better than a hot drink on a warm, cosy lounge in the middle of winter. What would a year be like without these extremes? Its the variety of experiences and feelings these two seasons' bring about that gives shape to our lives.

DAY 4

Choose which of the two conclusions below is more effective, and explain your decision.

COMEDY VERSUS DRAMA

Conclusion 1: While both comedy and drama are very different genres, they each possess qualities that make them enjoyable for audiences. Comedy is often the favoured genre for those who need a break from a hard day or for those who just want to have a good laugh with friends. Drama, on the other hand, is great when you want to immerse yourself in a thrilling story and engage with interesting characters.

Conclusion 2: We've discussed comedy and drama, so now let's take a look at some other genres. My personal favourite is horror. It's great to watch a horror movie on Halloween, and movies of this genre give you fun ideas for scary costumes. But if you're someone who gets scared easily, then horror might not be for you.

Explanation: ____

____

____

DAY 5

❶ **Edit this conclusion to a persuasive piece by correcting the three plural errors and the three apostrophe errors (two in the wrong place, one missing).** The previous paragraph of this text is on page 87.

THE RISKS OF SOCIAL MEDIA USE

In conclusion, though there is various risks that go along with using social media, there are safe ways for users to engage with one another. Teenage users should be aware of the dangers of cyberbullying and ask for help from adults if theyre unsure what to do. People should realise that cyberbullying are just as real and serious as bullying in the schoolyard. Users should also remember that social media enables people to present a picture of themselves that is not necessarily accurate or realistic. Ignoring individuals who you suspect are presenting a fake version of their live's is sometimes the best solution to this problem. Employing strategies like these can help to keep users' safe and ensure a positive experiences when using social media.

❷ **Write a conclusion for the topic you wrote about in Week 27, Day 5, Question 2. Remember to sum up the points you made without introducing any new material.**

____

____

____

____

____

____

____

____

____

DAY 1

Edit the imaginative piece below by correcting the six quotation mark errors (two in the wrong place, four missing). The previous part of this story is on page 88.

THE TEST

The sound of sharp, deliberate knocking woke Tristan the following morning. He slumped out of bed, his *Naruto* bedspread falling to a heap on the floor. He trudged to the door and opened it to reveal an unexpected visitor.

Flora!' he exclaimed. 'What are you doing here?'

'Tristan, I'm so sorry for last night. I shouldn't have called you a freak. I was just so scared. 'But friends are supposed to be there for each other no matter what.'

'I forgive you, Tristan said. But only because you're shouting breakfast, right?

'LOL! After what I did, that sounds fair,' Flora said. 'So tell me, do your hands feel hot when it happens?' Can you control it? I want to know all about your powers!'

DAY 2

! The resolution to a story is where the main problem (i.e. the complication) is resolved, and is usually where the story ends.

1. **Invent different resolutions to the story above for each of the ending types below. The first one has been done for you.**

   a Unresolved ending: *Tristan wakes up and sees a text from Flora saying she needs more time to think about what happened.*

   b Unhappy ending: ____________________

   ____

   c Plot twist: ____________________

   ____

2. **Which ending type do you think is most effective for 'The Test'? Why?**

   ____

   ____

DAY 3

Edit the imaginative piece below by correcting the five verb errors. The previous part of this story is on page 89.

TO THE CIRCUS WE GO: SCENE IV

Olga interrupts Deni's trance.

Olga: Oi, you! Stop daydreaming. I just gotten you an audition!

Deni: What? But how?

Olga: Let's just say I've got a date with someone who likes pink-and-green suits … Now put your leotard on quickly. Everyone was waiting!

Deni, in her acrobat costume, performs her routine in front of the circus panel. Everyone applauds. Deni will run off stage to embrace her sister.

Deni: Oh my god! I did it. I can't believe I did it. All those years of training paid off.

Olga: I knew you would, Sis. They are sure to accept you after that awesome performance. But then we'll have another problem, won't we: told Mum and Dad you're moving out to joining the circus!

DAY 4

Write a resolution for each of the complications below.

Complication	Resolution
Jill temporarily loses her sight just before her music-school audition.	
Sam likes Cleo but is not allowed to date until his grades improve.	
Ramon and his family get lost in the jungle.	
Mary time-travels to the future and is taken prisoner.	

Daily WRITING & EDITING Practice

DAY 5

❶ **Edit the imaginative piece below by correcting the three quotation mark errors (two in the wrong place, one missing) and the three verb errors.** **The previous part of this story is on page 90.**

TREASURE ADVENTURE

The two adventurers nod, confirmed their foolproof plan. Bjorn dug into his backpack and pulls out three cooked beef sausages while Mahesh waves furiously at the lion.

'Hey, big ugly lion!' Mahesh screams. Come and get me.'

'Mahesh races to the left and the lion starts chasing him. Bjorn, meanwhile, runs directly into the heart of the castle, towards the treasure. Out of the corner of his eye, the lion sees Bjorn running and changes direction, as agile as a gazelle.'

Using all his force, Bjorn throws the sausages as high into the air as he can. The lion's heads all turn upwards and lose focus on their former prey. Bjorn and Mahesh quickly rush into the castle and saw a tower of gold coins awaiting them.

❷ **Complete your imaginative piece from Week 28, Day 5, Question 3 by resolving the complication you set up in Week 26, Day 5, Question 2.**

DEVELOPING A VOICE

Daily checklist

WEEK	DAY 1	DAY 2	DAY 3	DAY 4	DAY 5
31	☐	☐	☐	☐	☐
32	☐	☐	☐	☐	☐
33	☐	☐	☐	☐	☐
34	☐	☐	☐	☐	☐
35	☐	☐	☐	☐	☐
36	☐	☐	☐	☐	☐
37	☐	☐	☐	☐	☐
38	☐	☐	☐	☐	☐
39	☐	☐	☐	☐	☐
40	☐	☐	☐	☐	☐

DAY 1

Edit the piece of personal writing below by correcting the six spelling errors.

MY FIRST DAY AT SECONDARY SCHOOL

My hart was pounding from the moment I got up this morning. Why? Because it was my first day at secondary school! I jumped out of bed like a bouncey kangaroo, put on the school uniform I had lade out the night before and raced to the bus stop. All the other kids on the bus seemed nervise, so no-one did much talking. Once we got to class, each of us was paired up with another student to be our buddy for the day. I was paired with the funnyest kid in class. I can already tell we're going to be good friends! Oh, and did I tell you about Miss Nichols, my homeroom teacher? She's the nicest, smartest person I've ever met. Today was the best! I can't wait for tommorrow.

DAY 2

! An informal voice is often used when writing about personal things. It is similar to the voice used in a casual conversation.

1. **Rewrite the sentences below using an informal voice. The first one has been done for you.**

   a I look forward to meeting you next week. *See you next week.*

   b How do you do? ______________________

   c I would be grateful if you would reply as soon as you are able.

   ____

   d I am writing to inform you that, unfortunately, I will not be able to attend.

   ____

2. **Using an informal voice, write a short summary of your first day at secondary school.**

____

____

____

____

____

Daily WRITING & EDITING Practice

DAY 3

Edit the piece of personal writing below by correcting the five comma errors (three in the wrong place, two missing).

MY FAMILY

My name is Sinag and I'm a Filipino Australian, who was born in Darwin Northern Territory. Both of my parents were born in the Philippines one in Manila and the other in Pasay. My mum's a typical Filipino mum. Even though she has a full-time job, as a criminal lawyer, she still finds time to do all the cooking – she makes the best adobo ever! – and to spend time with me. We do jigsaw puzzles and sing karaoke all the time. My dad's a freelance writer, so he works from home and spends even more time with me. We'll often shoot hoops at the local park and catch a movie at the cinema. On Saturdays, all three of us, will go visit my grandparents and take them out for lunch.

DAY 4

Complete the family tree below for your family (or for a fictional family). Using an informal voice, write a sentence describing each family member.

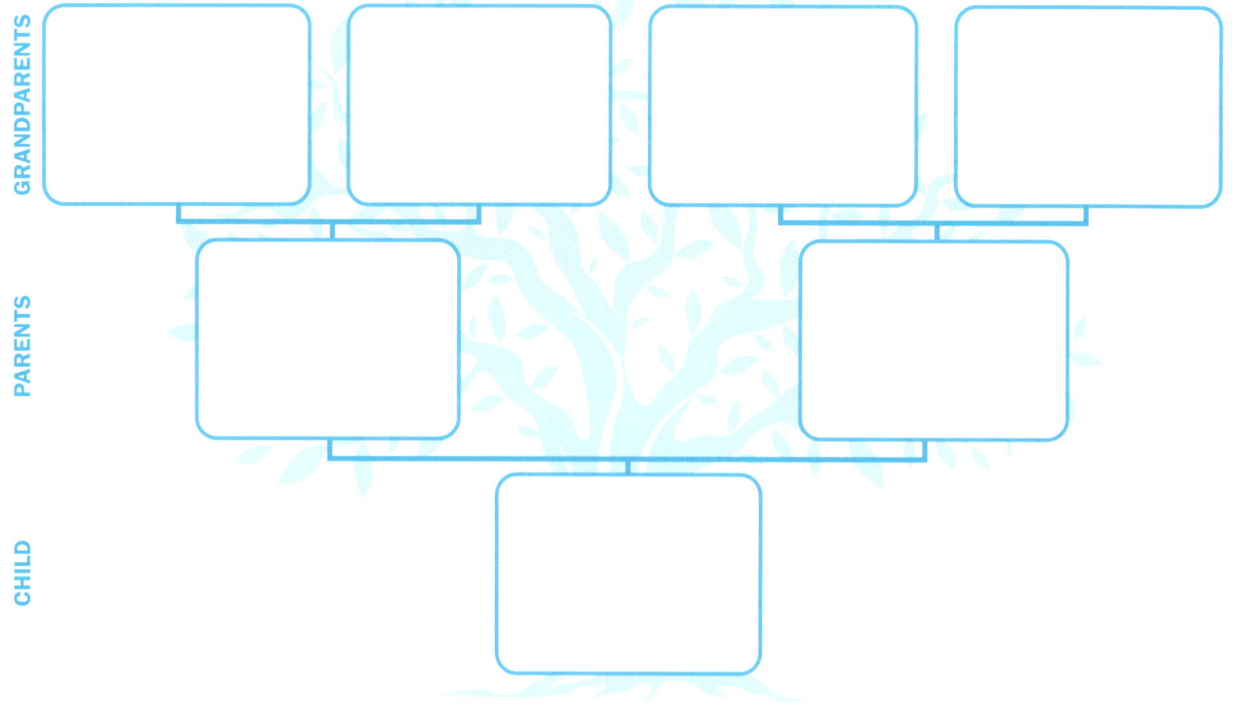

DAY **5**

❶ **Edit the piece of personal writing below by correcting the three spelling errors and the three comma errors (two in the wrong place, one missing).**

WHEN I GROW UP

When I grow up, I'm going to be a famous comedian. More famous than even Rebel Wilson or Jerry Seinfeld! I'm going to move to Hollywood and do stand-up shows, in all the famous comedie clubs. People will love my dry, sense of humour and hilarious impressions of celebrities. I do the best Arnold Schwarzenegger! After a few years of this, I'll be discovered by a TV execuetive and be given my own prime-time series. Kind of like *The Tonight Show*, but even funnier. I'll eventuelly return home and open up a school to teach young people how to be comedians telling them that making others laugh and smile is the best job in the world.

❷ **Using an informal voice, write a paragraph on the topic below.**

WHEN I GROW UP

DAY 1

Edit the letter below by correcting the seven plural errors.

TO MY LOCAL REPRESENTATIVE

Dear Minister,

I am writing to you in regard to the issues of renewable energy. Last month you and your government announced that you would provide individual with financial assistance to help install solar panels on their roofs. In addition, you agreed to build fifty new wind turbine by the end of the years. However, this week you announced that only some individuals would receive financial assistances, and only twenty wind turbines would be built. This latest announcement indicate that you do not recognise the importances of supporting renewable energy. I strongly advise you to commit to the changes you promised us and invest in the future of our children.

Yours sincerely,

Jan Nguyen

DAY 2

A formal voice uses language precisely and correctly. It can suggest the writer is being impersonal and objective.

1. **Highlight three formal phrases in the letter above.**
2. **Rewrite the sentences below using a formal voice. The first one has been done for you.**

a I think you've stuffed up! Change it now! *It is my opinion that you have made an error. Please make immediate changes.*

b Hey bro, what's up? Heard from your gramps lately? __________

c We pigged out like crazy last night! Never again! __________

d Thanks a lot – get back to me about next week ASAP. __________

DAY 3

Edit the cover letter below by correcting the eight capitalisation errors.

TO WHOM IT MAY CONCERN

I wish to apply for the position of professional sleeper at morningside grand Hotel. I believe I have the skill set, the experience and, most importantly, the positive attitude to excel in this role. my previous role as a product tester required me to identify how particular items could be improved, and I plan to bring the same level of Attention to Detail to this role, to ensure that your beds are the best in the industry.

I am excited about the possibility of working for your company in this dynamic role and would greatly appreciate the opportunity to make a positive contribution if given the chance. Thank you for your time and consideration.

Yours Sincerely,

gary angelous

DAY 4

Fill in the gaps to complete the cover letter for your dream job. Remember to write using a formal voice.

To whom it may concern,

I wish to apply for the position of ______________________________ at your company.

I believe I have the necessary skills to excel in this role. These skills include ______________

____.

I am passionate about working in this industry because ______________________________

____.

In closing, ____

____.

Yours faithfully,

____

DAY 5

❶ **Edit the letter below by correcting the three plural errors and the three capitalisation errors.**

AN OPEN LETTER

dear fellow citizens,

I am writing to you regarding a very important issue. Our oceans and the precious marine species that inhabit them is under attack from plastic pollution. Plastic garbage that humans dispose of decomposes slowly and entangles and kills tens of thousand of marine animals each year. It is important that human do their part to reduce plastic pollution. this can be achieved by using reusable water bottles and shopping bags, limiting the use of hard plastics, and Recycling whenever possible. The small changes can sometimes make the biggest impact, so let us work together to save our oceans and our fellow creatures.

A concerned citizen

❷ **Using a formal voice, write a letter to your school principal on a topic of your choice.**

Dear Principal,

____

____

____

____

____

____

____

____

Yours sincerely,

____

DAY 1

Edit this speech to a class by correcting the seven comma errors (four in the wrong place, three missing).

CLASS CAPTAIN NOMINATION

Good morning everyone,

I would like to nominate myself, for the position of class captain. As most of you know, I am hardworking reliable and honest. I feel that I am ready to take on more responsibility. I like to take the lead in making things happen. How many of you have been frustrated by the lack of recycling bins, around the school? Do you like me think that our canteen foods have, too, much plastic wrapping? I'd like to get all of your thoughts on small but important changes that would improve our school.

I hope you will consider voting for me as class captain. Thank you.

DAY 2

Knowing your audience will help you to choose appropriate language and whether to use a formal or an informal voice.

1. **Rewrite the following statements as if you are addressing your classmates. The first one has been done for you.**

   a Students are given too much homework.

   I'm sure you feel that we all get too much homework.

   b Teenagers would benefit from a later start to the school day.

   ____

   c Students should have a say in running the school.

   ____

2. **Circle the best expressions to use when the audience includes the teacher as well as the other students.**

   Good morning / Hi everyone. This is what I reckon / think we should do for our class party. First, hire a DJ. I recommend JoCool. He's very professional / awesome. Second, get / ask the Village Cafe to do the catering; their stuff / food is delish / delicious. Thank you / Thanks for listening.

DAY 3

Edit the letter to the editor below by correcting the five verb errors.

MAKE HOME COMPOSTING PART OF THE SOLUTION

I agree with the suggestion that we should all do more to reduce the amount of waste going to landfill (Letters, 3/10). Before we began home composting, my family fills several plastic bags each week with food scraps. Now these scraps go into our large green compost bin. Thought about how much food waste you throw in the bin each week. By my calculations, if every household will compost their food waste it would save around 20 litres of rubbish a week, for roughly 100 000 households per shire. That's over 100 megalitres each year! Perhaps councils could gave a free compost bin to each house to promoting this simple but highly effective means of reducing waste.

Mai Jones, Greenway

DAY 4

1. **Highlight two phrases in the letter above that show the writer is addressing adult readers who are responsible for running a household.**
2. **Fill in the gaps to complete a letter to the editor that responds to the one above. Use a formal voice and language suitable for a general adult audience.**

The idea that home composting can help to reduce landfill (Letters, 5/10) is ____________

______________________________ . I live in a ______________________________

with ______________ other people. We throw out around ______________________

of food waste each week. If we composted all this food waste, the impact it would have on our rubbish would be ______________________________ . For this reason, I would argue that ______________________________

____

____ .

DAY 5

❶ **Edit the persuasive piece below by correcting the three comma errors (one in the wrong place, two missing) and the three verb errors.**

PARTY PRESENTATION

Mum and Dad, do you remember you promised I could have a party, when I turned thirteen? I knew we haven't talked about it for ages, but since it's next month I thought we should start making some plans. I don't want you to have to do all the work. I writing the invitations. And what about having it at Game Ace? It's a great venue: they do food and have games music and a dance floor. If we had twenty guests or more they'll include a free cake. I think twenty would be the perfect number: ten boys and ten girls. Great! Is there anything I've left out?

❷ **Write a persuasive piece in which you try to convince an audience to do something. Use language appropriate for your audience.**

Audience: ______________________________

____

____

____

____

____

____

____

____

____

____

____

____

DAY 1

Edit the informative piece aimed at children below by correcting the six spelling errors.

BRICK BY BRICK

LEGO, a type of building toy, is one of the most popular producks in the world. The colourful plastic building blocks that can be joined together to make objects such as houses and castels have been around for almost a hundred years. They weren't always made of plastic, though. At first, LEGO bricks were made from wood. Plastic blocks were not made until the 1950s. Gradually, different types of peaces, such as weels and human figures, were added.

There are three key reasons why LEGO blocks are still so popular. First, the design is simple and child-freindly. Second, playing with them helps to develop imagination and constructian skills. Third, they're just a lot of fun – for both children and adults.

DAY 2

! Knowing your audience will help you to choose the most relevant information to include.

1. **In what ways is the passage above written to appeal to its target audience?**

____

____

2. **Highlight the three statements about parks below that would be the most appropriate for an audience of children, then write a statement of your own for this audience.**

- Parks improve the local tax base and increase property values.
- Parks often have playgrounds where you can play with your friends.
- Parks and recreation generate money for the local economy.
- Access to parks has been strongly linked to reductions in crime.
- Parks are the perfect place to have picnics with your family.
- Playing with your pets at the park can be super fun.

Statement: ____

____

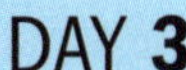

DAY 3

Edit the informative piece aimed at adults below by correcting the six plural errors.

THE LEGO COMPANY

The LEGO company is one of the oldest family-owned company in the world. It was founded in Billund, Denmark, in 1932. Its earliest toys was made from wood, but the company purchased a machine for injecting and moulding plastic in the 1940s. Gradually, LEGO piece became more diverse, as wheels and human figures were added to the range.

Today, LEGO pieces and sets is designed to appeal to all age groups, from young children to adults. One of the largest objects able to be made from a LEGO set are the Imperial Star Destroyer from *Star Wars* – this set contains 4784 pieces. There are also remote-controlled train sets and sets that involves coding and robotics, supporting science, technology and maths programs in schools.

DAY 4

1. **How does the passage above differ from the passage in Day 1?**

____

____

2. **Write a short piece addressed to an audience of adults on the benefits of parks.**

____

____

____

____

____

____

____

____

DAY 5

❶ **Edit the informative piece aimed at teenagers below by correcting the three spelling errors and the three plural errors.**

A DIGITAL BRICK EMPIRE

LEGO has come a long way since its creation in the 1930s. While it is best known as a producer of physacle building toys for kids, it has expanded into many other area since the turn of the century. This includes branching out into the digital worlds, bringing LEGO into the twenty-first century.

The most notable example of this is *LEGO Worlds*, a multiplayer video game in which players is able to bild an online world made up of LEGO bricks. Available on all major gaming systams (e.g. PlayStation 4, Xbox One and Nintendo Switch), *LEGO Worlds* shows how LEGO can remain on trend for generations to come.

❷ **Why would this passage appeal specifically to an audience of teenagers?**

____

____

❸ **Write a short piece on the topic in Day 4, Question 2. This time, make your piece appeal to an audience of teenagers.**

____

____

____

____

____

____

____

____

DAY 1

Edit the speech below by correcting the six capitalisation errors.

IF I WON THE LOTTERY

Wouldn't you love to win the lottery, fellow classmates? What would you do with the money if you did? Well, if i won the lottery, I would be over the moon with excitement! Firstly, I would place a portion of the money in my savings account, so that when i'm older I could use it to buy a house or an apartment to live in. Secondly, I would donate some of the money to important causes, such as animal welfare, youth homelessness and curing Cancer. Thirdly, I would spend some of the money on exciting adventures. for example, I would take my two sisters and my dad on an overseas holiday to egypt to visit Relatives I have never met.

DAY 2

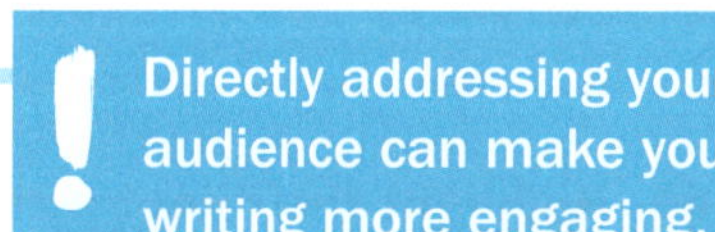

! Directly addressing your audience can make your writing more engaging.

1. **Highlight the direct address to the audience in the passage above.**
2. **Write a sentence that uses direct address for the scenarios below. The first one has been done for you.**

   a Paulo responds to a marriage proposal.

   Yes, my love, I'll marry you.

   b Stefan apologises to the teacher for being late.

   ____

   c You ask your mum for a snack.

   ____

   d Grace addresses the Prime Minister in a letter.

   ____

   e You tell your sibling to stop cheating.

   ____

DAY 3

Edit the speech below by correcting the four ending punctuation errors.

WHO IS MY HERO?

Mr Iyagi, I would like to tell you about my hero? My hero is selfless, generous and hardworking My hero is someone who puts the needs of others before his own. My hero wants the best for the people in his community. He does everything in his power to keep them safe and protect them from evil. My hero is mentally and physically strong; he doesn't need to rely on superpowers to achieve greatness, My hero fights for justice each and every day. My hero wants the world to be a better place for everyone The person I admire the most, my hero, is my brother Barton, the best police officer this town has ever known.

DAY 4

1. **Highlight the direct address in the passage above.**
2. **Fill in the gaps to complete a speech directed at your hero.**

You are my hero, ________________________ . Do you know why? Well, there are three reasons. The first reason is ____ .

The second reason is ____ .

The third reason is ____ .

Now you know why you, ________________________ , are my hero.

DAY 5

❶ **Edit the speech below by correcting the three capitalisation errors and the three ending punctuation errors.**

THE BEST THING ABOUT MY SCHOOL

Fellow classmates, the best thing about our school is that everyone who goes here is accepted for who they are. The teachers understand that each student is an individual with unique interests, The student welfare officer, ms cannon, works hard to make sure that all of us feel welcome. She organises student-bonding activities such as bake sales and open mic nights, so that going to school feels like being part of a great community another excellent thing that our school does is celebrate things like R U OK?Day and Wear it Purple Day, which shows our support for students in our school who are going through personal challenges

❷ **Write a speech to your parents outlining the best thing about your school. Include at least one example of direct address in your speech.**

____

____

____

____

____

____

____

____

____

____

____

____

DAY 1

Edit the speech below by correcting the four ending punctuation errors.

THE WORST CHORE

The chore that I dislike most is vacuuming, There is simply nothing enjoyable about it. Plus, I never get enough pocket money for doing it My sister always gets out of it because she is too small to vacuum properly, which leaves it up to me. It might sound like an easy chore but my mum insists that I remove everything from the floor to vacuum, then put everything back in its place. It takes hours And the dust that comes out of the old carpet gets up my nose and makes me sneeze. It really sucks. Do you know what the worst part is. Each time I vacuum, the dog tracks in mud and grass and then I have to do it again!

DAY 2

! Rhetorical questions do not require an answer from the audience. They are used to emphasise a point or make the audience think.

1. **Highlight the rhetorical question in the passage above. What do you think the purpose of this rhetorical question is?**

____

____

2. **Decide whether the questions below are likely to be rhetorical (R) or not (N).**

a What is the difference between a frog and a toad? R / N

b Do I look like I was born yesterday? R / N

c What's not to like? R / N

d Are there parent–teacher interviews tomorrow? R / N

e Did you put my favourite jumper in the wash? R / N

f Who doesn't love chocolate? R / N

g How could you do this to me? R / N

DAY 3

Edit the speech below by correcting the six apostrophe errors (four in the wrong place, two missing).

MY FAVOURITE PLACE IN THE WORLD

Have you ever been in complete awe of a place? We'll, thats the feeling I get when I go to the Warburton Redwood Forest. Its my favourite place in the world! The first thing you notice is the sound of bird's flitting through the trees. In the distance, you can hear the trickle of the river over rocks and logs. When you enter the forest you immediately feel calm. The redwood trees' tower over you, filtering the sunlight through their canopy of green. The trees are evenly spaced in every direction, so it feels as if there are endless paths to explore. The leaves and twigs crunch under your feet and the smell of damp earth fill's your nostrils. It's the best place to be.

DAY 4

Fill in the gaps in the conversation below to complete the rhetorical questions. The first one has been done for you.

A: I can't believe you went to the Warburton Redwood Forest without me! Did you really

think that I wouldn't find out?

B: I didn't mean to hurt your feelings, I swear. It's just that I really enjoy going there by myself. Just to go and think. Who doesn't ______________________________?

A: I guess that makes sense. But why didn't you just tell me that to begin with?

B: Because I didn't want to hurt your feelings. Haven't you ever ______________________________

______________________________?

A: You make some valid points, I suppose. What's the point ______________________________

______________________________?

B: You should go and enjoy the forest by yourself some time. It's so relaxing! Why not

______________________________?

DAY 5

❶ **Edit the speech below by correcting the three comma errors (one in the wrong place, two missing) and the three ending punctuation errors.**

THE NICEST THING THAT'S HAPPENED TO ME

Do you remember the nicest thing someone has done for you! I certainly do? It was when my best friend Hayat cheered me up by organising a class party for me at school. I was sad because Wentworth my cat had died the week before. Hayat asked our classmates to help by decorating our classroom with streamers and balloons, and she even made cupcakes for everyone. She's the nicest friend ever! Our teacher, Mr Anderson, also ran some games for us, such as 'Wink Murder' and 'Nemo'. It was so much fun. Everyone had such a great time together that it took my mind off Wentworth Even though I still miss him, it always makes me feel better, when I think about how my friends helped to cheer me up.

❷ **Write a speech about the nicest thing that has happened to you. Include a rhetorical question and at least one example of direct address in your speech.**

DAY 1

Edit the informative piece below by correcting the six verb errors.

MY SEARCH FOR THE TASMANIAN TIGER

The Tasmanian tiger is considered extinct. But some believe there are still tigers hiding out in the bush. I will spend a week in the Tasmanian wilderness, hunting for this elusive creature. I kept a journal of my experiences.

Day 1: I will follow a set of animal prints leading to a river, where I waited all day, watching. But no luck spotted a tiger.

Day 4: Stumbling across a rabbit's carcass, I saw teeth marks in its neck that resembled those of a tiger. That night, a pair of gleaming green eyes in the darkness startling me. I will grab my camera, but the creature disappeared before I could take the shot.

Day 7: The tracks have disappeared. The bush is silent. It's time to go home. Perhaps the Tasmanian tiger is still out there. But, if so, it clearly doesn't wishing to be found.

DAY 2

'Point of view' refers to the writer or narrator's perspective and voice. Three modes can be used: first person, second person or third person.

1. **Highlight two phrases in the text that are written in the first person. (The first-person point of view means using 'I' and 'me' to describe events, situations and feelings that are happening to the person writing.)**

2. **Write a first-person sentence using the following words: *looked*, *animal*, *disappointed*.**

___

___

3. **Write an alternative journal entry for Day 7 in which the narrator finds a Tasmanian tiger. Use the first-person point of view.**

___

___

___

DAY 3

Edit the instructional piece below by correcting the five spelling errors.

HOW TO SURVIVE IN THE BUSH

The Australian bush can be a dangerous place to get lost. But the following tips will help you survive until help arrives.

1 **Stay warm.** You should stuff your clothing with leafs to trap heat around your body.

2 **Find water.** Look for a lake or river and collect water from there. You can steralise it by leaving it out in the sun.

3 **Create a shelter.** It's important to be protected from both heat and rain. The easiest type of shelter to construct is with a collectian of leaves and branches.

4 **Stay put.** You have a much grater chance of being found by rescuers if you stay in one spot.

5 **Stay calm.** Panicing wastes energy and leads to bad decision-making.

DAY 4

1 **Rewrite the sentences below using the second person. (Writing in the second person means addressing the reader directly, using 'you'.) The first one has been done for you.**

a People can collect water from trees using plastic bags.

You can collect water from trees using plastic bags.

b Although I am scared of snakes, I must remain calm.

____

c I should remember to stay close to my friends.

____

2 **Using the second person, write a new tip for surviving in the bush.**

____

____

____

DAY 5

1 Edit the news article below by correcting the three verb errors and the three spelling errors.

MYSTERY SURROUNDS BUSH DISAPPEARANCE

Police are baffled by the sudden and mysterious dissappearance of a Melbourne student while on a school excursion on Tuesday. Thirteen-year-old Evie Ferguson is on a day trip to Hanging Rock in north-western Victoria when she vanished.

The group of students was following a well-marked trail and wheather conditions were good. Near the top of the rock, the path narrows so that hikers must travell in single file. Evie was at the head of the group. Classmates recall seeing her turn a corner, but when they will follow just seconds later, she was gone. Rescuers find no trace of the schoolgirl.

2 News articles are usually structured around answering the 'five W' questions. Answer the questions below based on the information in the text.

What happened? ____________________

Who did it happen to? ____________________

When did it happen? ____________________

Where did it happen? ____________________

Why did it happen? ____________________

3 Write a short news article about a made-up event. Use the third person. (Writing in the third person means using 'he', 'she', 'they' and people's names to refer to the individuals.)

DAY 1

Edit the imaginative piece below by correcting the seven comma errors (four in the wrong place, three missing).

DETECTIVE RIVALRY

I've had enough of smarty-pants, Rowena McKenzie my archenemy. She thinks she's such a good detective. But she's nothing compared to me. Everyone in town thinks Rowena is so clever just because she solved the mystery of Lucinda Mr Novinsky's missing cat. That's child's play, though. Is there anything more clichéd, than a cat stuck up a tree? I'm thinking big league here.

The identity of the ghost of Moon Hollow, is one of this town's greatest unsolved mysteries – unsolved until I came along, that is! I'm going to blow this case wide open proving to everyone that I'm the best detective around. Tomorrow morning I'll go down into the sea caves where the ghost is rumoured to have come from and start looking for clues. Let's see Rowena try and beat me, this time!

DAY 2

Point of view in imaginative texts is the narrative voice through which a story is told. When you write a story, you must decide who is telling it.

1. **Highlight three sentences that use the first person in the passage above.**

2. **Identify and explain which point of view (first, second or third person) is the most appropriate for each idea.**

   a a letter from your doctor giving you health advice **POV:** ☐ 1st ☐ 2nd ☐ 3rd

   Explanation: ____________________

   b a couple breaks up, but they decide to remain friends **POV:** ☐ 1st ☐ 2nd ☐ 3rd

   Explanation: ____________________

   c a diary entry about a bad experience at school **POV:** ☐ 1st ☐ 2nd ☐ 3rd

   Explanation: ____________________

DAY 3

Edit the imaginative piece below by correcting the five apostrophe errors (three in the wrong place, two missing).

CHOICES

You stand in a dimly lit corner of a deserted car park. A shadow looms into view. Youre filled with a sense of dread. You:

A walk toward's the figure

B find somewhere to hide

You choose A.

Its probably one of your friend's playing a trick, you think to yourself as you step forward bravely. As you approach the figure, you see that it's a tall woman with an intense gaze. She offers' you a chocolate bar, in exchange for a favour. You:

A take the chocolate bar and agree to the favour

B decline and walk away

You choose A.

DAY 4

Continue the imaginative piece above using the second person.

____

____

________________________________ . You:

A ____________________________

B ____________________________

You choose ____ .

____

____ .

DAY 5

1 Edit the imaginative piece below by correcting the three comma errors (one in the wrong place, two missing) and the three apostrophe errors (two in the wrong place, one missing).

AS SMALL AS ANTS

Piper and Cole suddenly began to shrink. One second they were normal teenager-sized human's the next they were the size of ordinary field ants. The uncut grass of their front lawn was now a scary and dangerous jungle, to them.

'Whats happening?' yelled Piper, her face contorted in fear.

Cole was speechless. He couldn't believe that he and his sister had shrunk. There was absolutely no explanation for them shrinking. Which meant they had no idea how to unshrink themselves.

A bloodcurdling chirp sounded through the blades of grass. Piper and Cole turned around and saw a giant ant scuttling towards them its mandible's ferociously gnawing at the air …

2 Write a short imaginative piece using one of the prompts below.

- a first-person account of a character who discovers they have magic powers
- instructions in the second person explaining how to respond to an alien invasion
- a third-person story about two siblings who have a fight

____

____

____

____

____

____

____

____

____

DAY 1

Edit the advertisement below by correcting the seven plural errors.

BUY NOW: *ALL BLACK*

All Black by Australian artist Tahnee is a stellar pieces of art that all art collectors will be dying to get their hands on! Tahnee has already proven herself as a rising star in the Australian art community, but this new painting will cement her as *the* voice of a generations. Eclipsing the highs of her previous works, *All Black* asks viewer to think about what arts really is. The entire canvas is black, allowing viewers to interpret the artist's intention in their own way. This piece of art sing with purpose. No other artist have dared to do something so bold, and Tahnee pulls off the feat with grace. Her new paintings is nothing short of remarkable.

DAY 2

> **!** The tone of a piece of writing shows the writer's emotions or attitude towards the subject.

1. **Sort the tone words below into the appropriate columns.**

passionate | calm | celebratory | worried | critical | serious | enthusiastic | disappointed | detached

Negative	Neutral	Positive

2. **Which of these tone words best describes the passage above?** ______________

3. **What do you think is the purpose of the passage, and how does the tone help the writer to achieve this purpose?**

____

____

DAY 3

Edit the review below by correcting the five ending punctuation errors.

REVIEW: *ALL BLACK*

Australian artist Tahnee's latest artwork, *All Black*, is an utter joke While no-one can deny the talent of this up-and-coming Australian painter – her portrayal of the Kimberley region of Western Australia in her first work is stellar – she has failed to hit the mark this time around, *All Black* is, as the title would suggest, nothing but a canvas covered in black paint. Where is the imagination! Where is the artist's personality. Perhaps she is trying to make some grand statement, but I don't see it, and that's a problem. Not only is this piece uninspired, it is also poorly executed. The harsh brushstrokes provide an uneven coat, suggesting the artist was rushing to complete it in time All in all, Tahnee's piece is very disappointing.

DAY 4

1. **How is the tone of the review above different from that of the passage in Day 1? What does the tone of this review suggest is the writer's purpose?**

   ____

   ____

2. **Write about a piece of art (this could include a film or a book) using the different tones below.**

   Enthusiastic: ____

   ____

   ____

   Critical: ____

   ____

   ____

DAY 5

1. **Edit the analytical piece below by correcting the three plural errors and the three ending punctuation errors.**

AN ANALYSIS OF *ALL BLACK*

Tahnee's *All Black* is a contemporary Australian artworks. It is a totally black painting that shun the traditional for more abstract ideas Unlike traditional artworks, which depict a particular scene, *All Black* seems to ask the viewer to do some thinking work. Perhaps the painting is a commentary on the trials faced by the Indigenous population in Australia, who may feel as though they are not seen as individuals in society. The thick and uneven brushstrokes could reflect the feelings of anger and fear that such people share, or they could represent the long and storied history of their ancestors? The exact meaning of this artwork is not immediately clear. And that seems to be the purposes of the artist: to make viewers decide the meaning for themselves,

2. **Identify the tone and purpose of the passage above.**

Tone: ______________________________

Purpose: ______________________________

3. **Write about the same piece of art you wrote about in Day 4. Choose the appropriate tone word below to achieve the purpose you decide on.**

Tone: angry mocking sentimental

Purpose: ______________________________

____

____

____

____

____

____

Daily WRITING & EDITING Practice

DAY 1

Edit the imaginative piece below by correcting the five apostrophe errors (one in the wrong place, four missing).

HIDING A SECRET

'Parminder, you wont believe it!' Willow screamed. 'I got us two ticket's to see Lola perform live!'

Parminder set down her milkshake and stared at her best friend in shock. She dropped to her chair as the shopping centre around her began to blur. 'What? … But how?' Parminder stuttered.

'I entered the concert lottery and won! Why aren't you jumping up and down more? You love Lola as much as I do. Shes all we ever talk about!'

Afraid she would reveal her closely guarded secret, Parminder mustered all her strength and began jumping around in feigned excitement. 'OMG! Youre right. This is great! Were finally going to see Lola on stage. I can't wait …'

DAY 2

! Using different points of view in an imaginative piece can reveal more aspects of a character.

1. **What do you think the voice of the narrator reveals about Parminder's character?**

____

____

2. **Write a short scene about a character, using the following first-person voice for the given purpose.**

   Voice: scared/worried **Purpose:** to show a character's vulnerability

____

____

____

____

____

DAY 3

Edit the imaginative piece below by correcting the five spelling errors.

PARMINDER'S DILEMMA

Parminder took the long route home, a millian thoughts tumbling through her mind. *This is the worse thing that could have possibly happened. If she goes to the concert, Willow is going to find out my secret. And if she does, then evarything will change. Forever. I won't be able to hang out with her anymore ... because she will never see me in the same way again. Plus, she won't be able to keep it a secret – not like I've been able to do all these years. If she tells someone at school, I'll have to move again! I can't let her go to that concert. I'll steel the tickets when she's not looking, or I'll preetend I'm sick. I'll do whatever it takes to protect my secret!*

DAY 4

1. **How does Parminder's internal voice in the passage above differ from the voice of the narrator of the passage in Day 1? What is the purpose of this change in voice?**

____

____

____

2. **Using the same character you wrote about in Day 2, write a short scene using the following voice for the given purpose.**

Voice: angry **Purpose:** to show how this character expresses their fears

____

____

____

____

____

____

DAY 5

❶ **Edit the imaginative piece below by correcting the three apostrophe errors (one in the wrong place, two missing) and the three spelling errors.**

IT'S LOLA

Parminder sat at her desk and began typing.

To the best fans in the whole world,

Lola here. I wanted to write to you all personalley to say sorry about cancelling my show this Saturday night. I was totally looking forward to playing for you all, but I've come down with a terribal cold and can't sing.

That's a big fat lie: Im just scarred that my best friend, Willow, will discover that Ive hidden my secret identity from her for so long.

Parminder shook her head, deleted the last sentence and continued typing.

I hope I can come back to your town in a few month's to perform. We're going to party so hard!

Love and kisses,

Your fav, Lola ♥

❷ **Using the same character you wrote about in Days 2 and 4, write a short scene. Select a different voice and purpose for this scene to show another side to your character.**

Voice: ____________________ **Purpose:** ______________________________

____

____

____

____

____

____

____

____

PERSUASIVE WRITING PROMPTS

To practise your persuasive writing skills, write short pieces (around 400 to 600 words) on the topics below. See 'Unit 3: Structuring Responses' for tips on how to structure a persuasive piece of writing.

1 'Pets should be allowed in schools.' Do you agree?

2 Persuade your parents to let you redecorate your room.

3 Is chess a sport or a game?

4 'It is wrong to keep animals in zoos and use them in circuses.' Do you agree?

5 'Students should not be forced to take physical education classes.' Do you agree?

6 Is remote/online learning as effective as traditional classes?

7 Persuade your teacher to hold lessons outside.

8 Do hobbies help people with their careers?

9 'Every public place should have free wi-fi.' Do you agree?

10 'Having too many friends can be a bad thing.' Do you agree?

11 'Smoking should be banned in all public areas.' Do you agree?

12 Convince your friend to lend you their most prized possession.

13 Should students who commit cyberbullying outside of school be suspended?

14 'Life is better without computers.' Do you agree?

15 Write a letter to your local politician on a topic of your choice.

IMAGINATIVE WRITING PROMPTS

To practise your imaginative writing skills, write short pieces (around 400 to 600 words) on the topics below. See 'Unit 3: Structuring Responses' for tips on how to structure an imaginative piece of writing.

1 You wake up one morning and discover that your legs have turned into the tail of a fish.

2 Imagine you are an animal living in a zoo.

3 Write a story using these three words: *kite*, *enemy*, *laughing*.

4 Imagine how your parents met.

5 A friend gives you a lamp and you discover it contains a genie who will grant you three wishes.

6 You swap bodies with your teacher for the day.

7 Dolphins take over the world and humans must do as they say.

8 When you get to school, you are told that all the other students have gone missing.

9 A snowstorm hits your town and you are stuck in one place until it is over.

10 You've invented a time machine and visit your favourite period in history.

11 Write about a mistake that breaks up a friendship.

12 Imagine dinosaurs are still alive today.

13 Write a story using these three words: *storm*, *broom*, *blackout*.

14 Imagine you are a character in your favourite television show.

15 You discover a new land.